SOCIAL SECTOR HERO

How Government and Philanthropy Can Fund for Impact

ADAM LUECKING

with **Kayleigh Weaver**

Foreword by Dr. JaNay Queen Nazaire

SOCIAL SECTOR HERO

© 2022 Adam Luecking

ISBN 978-1-66785-630-8

eBook ISBN 978-1-66785-631-5

DEDICATION

This book is dedicated to the Clear Impact staff, past and present, whose talent and passion for measurable improvements and superior technology have inspired Social Sector Heroes across the globe.

PRAISE FOR SOCIAL SECTOR HERO

Adam is one of the top leaders in the worldwide Results-Based Accountability (RBA) community. In this important book, Adam brings new insights into the crucial role that funders play in measurably improving the quality of life in the communities they serve. Whether you are new to the concepts in this book or an experienced practitioner you will find useful advice and inspiring stories. I highly recommend it for both funders and their grantees.

– Mark Friedman, Director of the Fiscal Policy Studies Institute, creator of Results-Based Accountability, and author of *Trying Hard is Not Good Enough*

Social Sector Hero is a valuable manual, with easy-to-follow instructions on making the impact everyone in our sector dreams of making. As Adam states in Chapter Two, "No one entity can do this work in isolation." It takes all of us, and Adam's book helps light and direct a path forward. The book is a rich reminder that we can all be heroes.

– Kristin Hartley, Director of Organizational Impact, Child & Family Service, Hawai'i

If you're planning for or already on the journey to achieving population-level impact, this book is an indispensable road map. It's a terrific resource – filled with practical guidance and inspiring stories.

– Ron Fairchild, President and CEO, Smarter Learning Group

If you are in governmental public health, you will recognize stories about superheroes who separate population accountability from program account-ability. You understand that everyone must "do what you can with what you have." Adam's book provides practical advice on decreasing time spent

in meetings, learning to be concise, and staying focused on results. This is a must-read for public health professionals who work with wicked problems.

– Kathryn Dail, Director, Healthy North Carolina 2030, North Carolina Division of Public Health

Adam's book focuses on funders and organizational leaders and why the Results-Based Accountability approach makes sense from a funding perspective. The stories and recommendations Adam shares demonstrate practical and effective approaches that will work for real people, organizations, and communities around the world. This book is powerful reading for leaders and funders who want to make a difference.

– Anne McIntyre-Lahner, CEO of Action 2 Outcomes, former Director of Performance Management at Connecticut Department of Children and Families, and author of *Stop Spinning Your Wheels – Using Results-Based Accountability to Steer Your Agency to Success*

Adam busts a global myth in his latest book. Measuring impact isn't limited by geography, industry, or client group. Every community deserves our commitment and discipline to just start working in a different way.

– Julie Hourigan Ruse, CEO, SHINE for Kids (Australia)

You will see yourself in this book; perhaps, even, in one or more of these Heroes' journeys. Follow Adam's advice for getting started on your own journey and just do it. His entertaining, sensible approach and unassuming way will give you the confidence you need to start looking at performance and accountability in a different way and to push through any challenges that stand in the way of your work towards a Common Purpose.

– Marian Rueter Godwin, Director of Community Impact Services, United Way of Central Iowa

Tēnā koutou katoa (Greetings to you all). I am an indigenous wāhine (woman) of Aotearoa New Zealand. Māori are the indigenous peoples of our beautiful country. I have known and worked with Adam and the Clear Impact team for many years. I write this mihi (acknowledgment) because we have used RBA and the many techniques outlined in Adam's book for nearly a decade. As an indigenous consultancy firm that stands unapologetically for ōritetanga (equity), manawaroa (resilience), oranga (wellbeing) and tukunga iho (results), and in our own right as an indigenous provider of oranga | wellbeing services for all, we have worked with government, non-government organisations, Māori health, and social service providers and iwi (tribes) to apply RBA and use it to inform strategy, policy, service design, and delivery practices. Our approach to outcomes mahi (work) has always been to privilege tāngata (people), whānau (family), and hāpori (community) aspirations and then to activate 'turning the curve' in order to transform aspirations into reality. What we really value in Adam's book is that it aligns with our intent of peoples' wellbeing first, systems and services second. In other words, we are here to serve and activate people, family, community, and tribal aspirations and well-being not the other way around. Finally, as leaders of change and oranga | wellbeing, despite the many challenges Adam's book reminds us of, I encourage you to stick to the kaupapa (purpose). Sometimes you will feel discouraged that the 'machine' just won't or can't change. Our advice is to surround yourself with a network of passionate people who like you, want the very best for those who need our support the most. You will experience highs and lows but always remember that person, family, or community that you supported to be their own agents of change and who were, therefore, able to flourish themselves and go on to lead intergenerational wellbeing. I end with this whakatauki (proverb) from my culture – E hara taku toa i te toa takitahi, engari he toa takitini. My strength is not as an individual but that of the collective. I wish you the very best in your journey. Mauri ora.

– Sharon Shea MNZM, Owner and Principal Consultant, Shea Pita & Associates (New Zealand), Ngāti Ranginui, Ngāti Haua, Ngāti Hine, Ngāti Hako (Sharon's tribal affiliations)

TABLE OF CONTENTS

BEGINNING (OR CONTINUING) YOUR HERO'S JOURNEY

If you are reading these words, thank you. You have already taken the first step on your journey to become a Social Sector Hero — and we need more heroes in this space. The only way we'll get them is if people like you commit to the necessary steps it takes to bring results, accountability and high performance to our work in the face of overwhelming challenges.

When I began my hero's journey, I did not have the words to describe it, nor did I even realize it was a hero's journey. I just knew I wanted to make a measurable difference in people's lives across the world. Part of the journey has included time with Adam before and after he founded Clear Impact. Together, he and I worked on a project for the University of Maryland and the Annie E. Casey Foundation that convened public, philanthropic and nonprofit leaders working to achieve measurable outcomes for children and families across the state of Maryland.

Working with Adam, I began to see his unique approach to performance and accountability — and the difference it made for the communities and organizations he worked with. Once he started Clear Impact to help more communities, I joined him as a Senior Consultant, working with hundreds of organizations and communities in the U.S. and abroad to help them do their work better.

During those five years, I saw first-hand what it took to achieve and sustain large-scale results using the Clear Impact Scorecard and other tools. Working across numerous cities, counties, states and countries with Adam, I was continuously amazed by his ability to encourage our clients towards success despite the challenges they faced. I started to call him "Mr. Opportunity" because of his optimistic outlook. He has an uncanny talent for convincing people to do things and follow through on their commitments, no matter how big or small. This upbeat, dedicated attitude continues to be the archetypal element of a Social Sector Hero for me to this day, and I am thankful that this book offers the words, tools and insights that give meaning to the journey.

We can't all be Adam and his "Mr. Opportunity" alter-ego, but thanks to this book, we can learn from his extensive career and the communities he's worked with to achieve large-scale results. Often when I am facilitating a conversation about what it would take to shift population-level outcomes — such as growing businesses owned by people of color — there's resistance and hesitation to tackle the challenges head-on. When people start to break down the elements and necessary work to achieve these results, they just don't think it's possible. But Adam has proven it's possible and in this timely book, with its step-by-step instructions, Adam will teach you how to get from stuck to success on your results journey.

Before, during and after my time working with Adam, government and philanthropic funders were increasingly looking for nonprofits and organizations that had a results-driven mindset and were committed to high performance. This began in the fallout of the Great Recession, when we needed to do 'more with less', but it continued as our country's intractable problems — racism, climate change, income inequality — were increasingly exposed as the existential threat to our collective wellbeing that they are.

I left Clear Impact for Living Cities, a funder collaborative of the world's largest foundations and financial institutions. These were some of the largest private funders in the world — Ford Foundation, Gates Foundation, Wells Fargo, CitiBank — and my exposure to the challenges they faced in solving large-scale problems only confirmed the need for a dramatic shift across the social sector towards a results-oriented culture. Those that integrate a culture of inclusive high performance, based in humanity and multiple ways of learning, knowing and doing, will be rewarded; those that do not will struggle.

Ultimately, these funders are working toward the same goal: dramatic improvement in the conditions of wellbeing for people and communities. This book gives you the tools to get there — from securing alignment with partners to the necessary step of disaggregating data, from the need for qualitative storytelling to the importance of public accountability on your actions. As with most things, the lessons contained in these pages are easier said than done, but Adam's accessible writing, clarity of approach, and helpful case studies will make the implementation much easier.

Our country has its share of overwhelming challenges these days. In my career, I've seen the awareness of these challenges grow, with more and more people across industries stepping up to take on the burden that comes with being a Social Sector Hero. Thanks to the book you are now reading, I'm confident that heroes like you will be equipped to tackle the challenges we need to overcome as a country to ensure we can all thrive.

Dr. JaNay Queen Nazaire
June 2022.

INTRODUCTION:
THE SOCIAL SECTOR HERO'S JOURNEY

"You may encounter many defeats, but you must not be defeated. In fact, it may be necessary to encounter the defeats, so you can know who you are, what you can rise from, how you can still come out of it." – Maya Angelou

Hello, and thank you for opening up this book today. My name is Adam Luecking, and I am the co-founder and CEO of Clear Impact — a performance management software and services provider with roots in the bustling Washington, D.C. metro area.

As I sit down to write, Clear Impact has just celebrated its fifteenth birthday, and throughout this rewarding journey, I have had the privilege of working closely with governments, nonprofits, and philanthropic funders in a dozen different countries around the world.

This book is for the people I call 'Social Sector Heroes': The funders, grantees and teams that work so hard to care for our children, families and communities. All of the Social Sector Heroes I've worked with over the years are fiercely passionate about what they do. And that makes sense — you have to be extraordinarily passionate to take on this extraordinarily challenging work. I've met hundreds of Social Sector Heroes in the last 15 years, and a lack of passion or goodwill is never an issue.

Social Sector Heroes bring passion, discipline, and accountability to their work. A Social Sector Hero is not perfect and they have justifiable fears and strong emotions around their work; they have good days and bad days. At some point, they may even have felt hopeless or resigned about their ability to make a difference, because Social Sector Heroes are human beings. But despite their fears and challenges, a Social Sector Hero ultimately decides to keep pushing forward. They use setbacks as a learning opportunity, rather than an excuse to give up. Finally, a Social Sector Hero understands that they don't know everything, that it's OK to ask for help, and there is no such thing as perfect. They are open-minded and they do not let perfectionism prevent them from taking action.

But many social and public sector organizations struggle to turn that passion into tangible results and impact.

According to the National Philanthropic Trust, philanthropic funders (and the individual donors that make that philanthropic work possible) are spending an ever-increasing amount on promoting public wellbeing.[1] Just look at the numbers from a couple of years ago:

- Americans gave $471.44 billion in 2020, a 5.1 percent increase from 2019.
- Foundation giving in 2020 increased to $88.55 billion, a 19 percent increase from 2019.

---

1 https://www.nptrust.org/philanthropic-resources/charitable-giving-statistics/

Let's look at government funding. According to USASpending.gov, the Federal Government spent $7.5 trillion on grants and fixed charges in FY2021, comprising 74.5 percent of its spending.[2]

It's a similar story when it comes to nonprofits. Currently, there are at least 1.4 million nonprofits in the United States. Combined, nonprofits (including charities and foundations) spend nearly $2 trillion annually.[3] If you stacked $100 bills on top of each other, $2 trillion would reach 1,262 miles into space (and to put that into perspective, it only takes about 62 miles to leave Earth's atmosphere and enter suborbital space). We are quite literally spending an exorbitant amount of money.

So what's the problem? Why isn't all that money — and the vast reserves of time, energy and goodwill — being poured into our society's problems making a bigger difference?

We're spending billions and often trillions of dollars on the social good, and we have good data on these expenditures. But there is not an equal emphasis on providing data on the *impact* of that spending. Measuring the impact of philanthropic investments on wellbeing is much harder than analyzing spending (and the addition of a global pandemic in 2020 has complicated that even further).

The issue, as we've come to understand it, is that two key components are missing from the battle plan of most organizations: a Results-Based Accountability (RBA) strategy and scalable, repeatable systems that allow teams to reliably deliver on their mission.

Now, when we first meet Social Sector Heroes, the mere mention of words like 'Results-Based Accountability' can introduce a mild sense of panic into the room. Either that, or people start settling in for a nap. But

---

2 https://www.usaspending.gov/explorer/object_class

3 https://www.thenonprofittimes.com/news/80-of-nonprofits-revenue-is-from-government-fee-for-service/:

RBA is far more accessible than it sounds. Done correctly, it will not overwhelm you with data, nor is it another buzzword that sounds exciting but never delivers meaningful change.

I want to help your organization design a repeatable and scalable process to align your strategy and funding, analyze and improve your performance, establish productive dialogues with grantees, and — most importantly — improve the wellbeing of your customers and communities. To ensure flexibility, I have focused only on what I believe to be the most important steps and actions you'll want to take.

You've probably heard it countless times before: increasingly restrained budgets make data-based decision-making and investing more important than ever. It's never been more important to make the most effective budget, strategy, grant, and program implementation decisions possible, because nonprofits, government agencies, and public sector organizations find themselves in a pivotal moment in time. The COVID-19 pandemic has forced many organizations and businesses into a state of emergency that continues beyond the publication date of this book. While it's understandable that budgets have been slashed and funds are being funneled towards mitigation and recovery, it is also a time when demand for services is increasing and the industry is facing staff shortages — all of which creates an immense amount of pressure on the social sector and the people working in it.

And whether you call them objectives, goals, missions, outcomes, impacts or results, it's the difference you make that ultimately matters — not the amount you spend or even the number of people you reach. You can reach a lot of people with a program and make very little difference if the program isn't the appropriate solution to the problem.

The difference is the *impact* you get from your social investments: the measurable improvements in the organizations, communities, and/or individuals you aim to serve. Did you actually improve anyone's life, and to what degree?

Your measurable impacts are the most important pieces of data you and your grantees could ever possess or share. These are things like, "Percentage of job training program participants who get and keep living-wage jobs six months after completing the program." Any organization with any mission can create a measure like this; it doesn't matter what kind of programming you provide. If you're a funder, your grantees will probably do most of this measuring. Your role is to help standardize your grantmaking decisions using data, grantee impact reporting processes, and the actual measures used across similar funded programs.

RBA ideas can provide you and your team with clarity that will help you structure and scale your work for impact. These are ideas like "establish a clear, common purpose" or "use data to make decisions." These ideas are so universal that they span sectors, industries, and all types of organizations. They are fundamental business principles and are useful whether you're seeking profit, impact, or both.

You don't have to take my word for it, though. Throughout this book, you'll hear from sixteen Social Sector Heroes who have taken RBA and used it to absolutely transform their organization — and the lives of the people they serve.

I'm sure you will be able to relate to many of the stories in this book. Many of these organizations have faced inertia and inaction, usually stemming from (entirely justifiable) fears — like the fear that data will be used to punish and blame. These fears tend to manifest as resistance to change and end up being justifications for why previous efforts to introduce data and systems might not have worked:

1. Too expensive

2. Too time-consuming to set up

3. Too time-consuming to manage

4. Too burdensome on grantees to collect and report data

5. Too much pushback from grantees

6. Selecting measures is too difficult

7. Data is too difficult to find

These objections are just a handful of the obstacles that can present themselves on the Social Sector Hero's journey to impact. So whether you're overwhelmed with data, wasting time with duplication of efforts, struggling to get buy-in, or have no clue how to measure your and your grantees' impact, don't worry. I designed this book to help you overcome the challenges preventing you from truly understanding and maximizing the impact of your donors' dollars. I want to help you ensure your investments are generating results that improve the lives of your communities, by establishing a repeatable system that will make the difference between just trying hard and actually getting results.

When you can develop a clear and flexible system for results and accountability, you can be confident that you are making the best data-based decisions and investments.

Why "systems" and "flexibility"? They kind of seem like opposites, don't they? Well, systems make efforts repeatable, measurable, and scalable. Flexibility allows diverse people, groups, and circumstances to adapt systems to their unique assets, insights, and perspectives without blowing up the bridge to the original mission. Creating flexible systems is difficult, but you really need both to make the biggest difference: you need the most people possible to buy into your new way of operating if you want to achieve your mission, but if you're too rigid about the system, it will almost never work.

So how do you create flexibility? You focus more on the *ends*, rather than the *means*: more focus on *what* you want your staff and your grantees to accomplish, and less on the details and minutiae of *how* they accomplish it. This is what I want to help you figure out through the recommendations we will cover here.

This book cannot provide an exhaustive list of every single step you and your organization will need to follow. That part will be up to you, because every funder is different and will face different obstacles. But there are clear problem patterns I've come across that we will tackle: things like data paralysis, misalignment of efforts, inertia, and the inability to communicate your impact. In other words, I've focused on the biggest obstacles preventing your progress (the boulders instead of the pebbles, if you will).

There are also patterns among the most effective and most successful of the Social Sector Heroes that Clear Impact has worked with. That's why a large part of this book will highlight stories from some of our most impactful clients and customers — those we consider to be exemplary Social Sector Heroes — and what we have learned working with them.

RBA and RBA training play an important role in the majority of stories I'll share in this book. However, my advice is generally applicable to any framework. I will never demand that you use specific terminology exactly as I've laid it out. Instead, I'll tell you what has worked for many others like you, provide evidence and guidance, and then encourage you to find the power within yourself and your organization to make it happen.

Our Heroes' journeys are complex and sometimes span decades of effort that cannot be captured in a couple of pages. Like me, they don't want it to take decades for you to make a difference. Take what they offer and use it to accelerate your progress.

The stories and recommendations in this book will help you reduce the time it takes to create a world-class accountability and performance reporting system with your grantees. This system will...

1.   Add more value instead of burden

2.   Become repeatable and scalable by design

3.   Help you and your grantees create and communicate your measurable impacts.

I've worked to make the recommendations widely applicable to all kinds of readers, but detailed enough that you will be able to start implementing them right away.

If you've read my first book or seen the title — *The Holy Grail of Public Leadership and the Never-Ending Quest for Measurable Impact* — you'll know I'm a huge fan of adventure and fantasy stories. That's why I've structured this book as a kind of 'social impact journey' or hero's adventure. Just as many fantasy stories involve a fellowship of characters on a quest through a mythical land in search of treasure or transformation, so too does the Social Sector Hero's journey. You will need the skills of every person on your team, a clear mission, and more than a little luck to get to your desired destination. You'll face challenges throughout your hero's journey, and I believe the guidance in this book will help you overcome those tough moments and ongoing puzzles.

Imagine it this way: You and your grantees are on a journey through a mountainous landscape. At the top of the tallest mountain is a treasure (social impact). Along the path, there are obstacles like falling boulders (staff turnover), a broken bridge across a rushing river (misaligned reporting systems), a field of flowers emitting a sleep-inducing toxin (overwhelming amounts of data), and off in the distance, one-eyed giants are battling on the mountainside (mismatched political and operational interests).

You're completely stuck. You've approached the hazy field of flowers and have no idea how you're going to get through without everyone collapsing in a snoring heap. Then, you spot something — the corner of an old tattered scroll sticking out of the dirt behind a small boulder. The scroll was written long ago by a wizard who accompanied countless groups on their journey to the top of the mountain. In the scroll, the wizard has drawn instructions on how to use materials from the local landscape to fashion a magical mask. This tool will allow your group to pass through the field unharmed and reach the next stage in your journey.

I'm not saying I'm a wizard, and my advice isn't easy or a magic fix. But I hope this book can be a little like the scroll in the story for you and your colleagues. I want to help you reach the top of the mountain as fast as possible.

* * *

It is important for me to note that many of the recommendations offered within these pages are drawn from or inspired by the RBA framework, described in the book *Trying Hard is Not Good Enough,* by Mark Friedman. I consider this book a must-read supplement to your journey (Mark truly is a wizard). However, to help get you started, I will illustrate principles that apply no matter what frameworks you use. What you decide to call things is far less important to me than your actions and commitment. There are lots of approaches to impact.

Throughout this book, I will use RBA terminology when discussing certain concepts and sharing our Social Sector Hero stories. Here's a brief glossary of common RBA terms I will use to aid your understanding.

Glossary of Common RBA Terms You'll Come Across in This Book:

(adapted from *Trying Hard is Not Good Enough,* by Mark Friedman)

- **Population:** A particular group (or sub-group) of people defined by category and geography (e.g. "All children in the county," "All children 0 to 5 in the world," "All elders in the neighborhood," "All elders in the state with incomes below the poverty level").

- **Population Accountability:** Accountability for the wellbeing of a whole Population in a geographic area. Population Accountability is bigger than any one program or agency or single level of government. It requires the whole community, and public and private partners to make a difference. No one person or organization can be held accountable for the wellbeing of a Population.

- **Results:** Conditions of wellbeing for children, adults, families, and/or communities, stated in plain, preferably positive language: "Our community has adequate affordable housing for all people," "Our county's kindergarteners enter school ready to learn," "Our state's babies are born healthy."

- **Indicators:** A measure that helps quantify the achievement of a Result, such as "Poverty rate," "Infant mortality rate," "Percentage of kindergarteners who enter school ready to learn."

- **Performance Accountability:** Accountability for the performance of an organization, program, service, or service-system. As opposed to accountability for Populations, Performance Accountability is about organizing our work to have the greatest impact on our "customers" — the organizations, communities, and/or individuals we serve directly.

- **Programs/Services:** A program, agency, or service-system responsible for helping reach the stated Results. Programs are not themselves strategies; they are expressions of strategies. Programs are specific ways of implementing strategies, usually targeted toward a specific sub-group within the population. For example, a strategy of family support may have as one expression the program called Nurturing Families Network, which is targeted at new parents at risk of abusing or neglecting their newborn child.

- **Performance Measures:** Measures of how well public and private programs and agencies are working. The most important Performance Measures tell us whether the clients or customers of the program or service are better off. Measures that track the quality of the Program are also important here.

Performance Measures can apply to entire agencies, service delivery systems, or individual programs. An example might include, "the percentage of job training recipients that increase their wage or got a new job."

- **Strategies:** A coherent collection of actions that have a reasoned chance of improving Results. Strategies are made up of our best thinking about what works, and they include the contributions of many partners. No single action by any one agency can create the improved results we want and need.

- **Action Plan:** A set of actions, projects, or initiatives that are undertaken to improve an Indicator or Performance Measure. Actions within an Action Plan, as well as the Action Plan as a whole, should define start and end dates and the people responsible.

- **Turn the Curve Thinking:** The process of moving from the desired end state in the future (ends) to the steps we need today to get there (means). Specifically, turning a trend on a data graph from a negative direction to a positive direction. Turning the Curve describes efforts to improve the direction or rate of change in the baseline of an Indicator or Performance Measure. It is also a short-hand for the process of determining whether the current and projected level on an Indicator or Performance Measure is acceptable or requires change.

Thank you for promoting the wellbeing of children, families, and communities through your work. I hope you find this to be a valuable asset in your Social Sector Hero's quest for clear, measurable impact. With the contents of this book, I hope to empower you and your grantees to conquer your fears around data, overcome challenges and doubts, maximize your funding, and reach the peak of your impact journey faster.

CHAPTER 1:

MAGNIFICENT INTENTIONS

"Intent without dedicated action is simply not enough. Action without
a clear intent is a waste. It is when these two powerful forces are aligned
that the energy of the universe conspires in your favor."
– Steve Maraboli, *Life, the Truth, and Being Free*

It was the dawn of 1842. Charles Dickens, the nineteenth-century British author of famous works like *Oliver Twist*, *A Tale of Two Cities*, and *Great Expectations*, needed a rest. To rejuvenate, Dickens and his wife planned a six-month trip to America. But the trip wasn't just an escape from the stressors of public life. During his travels, he planned to advocate for international copyright laws; unauthorized reproductions of his work in the New World were not earning him the returns he was entitled to. As a dedicated social reformer, Dickens hoped American Democracy would make lawmakers and the public amenable to his cause.

Dickens approached his arrival in Boston with optimism. He possessed an idealistic image of America and hoped it would truly reflect what he deemed "the Republic of my imagination." But as the weeks flew by, he grew jaded by what he experienced. He began to find the adoring crowds to be increasingly aggressive and invasive.

His greatest disappointment was perhaps triggered during a stint in Washington, D.C. While he considered it well-intentioned, the actual functioning of American Democracy did not live up to his expectations. As for politicians, he came to view them as "a stream of desperate adventurers which sets that way for profit and for pay. It is the game of these men… to make the strife of politics so fierce and brutal, and so destructive of all self-respect in worthy men, that sensitive and delicate-minded persons shall be kept aloof, and they, and such as they be, left to battle out their selfish views unchecked."[4]

As a result, Dickens coined D.C. a "City of Magnificent Intentions." To him, Washington only claimed to represent a pinnacle of justice, ambition, and equality. What he witnessed instead was what he described as a land of opportunists that condoned slavery and participated in propaganda. In other words, the American operation was not living up to its confidently communicated intentions.

I'll spare you the rest of his scathing review, but the point here is that it is not enough to have good intentions. Our actions as public servants must reflect those intentions, and we must constantly ask ourselves whether we are living up to them. If we aren't, we must re-evaluate (with good and reliable data) and change course where necessary.

As my friend and colleague Mark Friedman says in *Trying Hard is Not Good Enough*, "It is about making a difference, not just trying hard and hoping for the best."

If you've entered public or social service, you have almost undoubtedly done so with great expectations and honorable intentions. But if you're reading this book, you've probably felt jaded at times — just like Dickens did — by what you've experienced. We need only to look at the increases in

---

4 https://library.georgetown.edu/exhibition/dickens-georgetown-bicentenary-celebration

philanthropic spending and passion among our friends and colleagues to get a sense that "trying hard enough" isn't the issue.

Not only should we be making a difference, but the difference must also be measurable. We must fall in love with the process of collecting, analyzing, and acting on data if we want to make a positive impact that lasts. We must humbly acknowledge where we are falling short. We must come to terms with the fact that intentions are meaningless without action.

Measuring your impact and that of your grantees will help you make better decisions. You'll be able to determine which programs are working, which might work better with some changes, and which are actually draining your resources with no measurable results. You'll be able to appropriately re-allocate resources and funding to the programs making the greatest impact, allowing you to accelerate towards your goals faster. Again, you'll be ensuring you're not just an organization of magnificent intentions but an organization of magnificent action and impact.

Now, as the funder, you're the backbone for the entire operation, but you must respect the unique skills, knowledge and resources of your grantees and their communities. You're kind of like Frodo in *The Lord of the Rings* — just as carrying the ring around his neck was a burden, so too is carrying the responsibility of helping your entire fellowship reach its destination. You are an important part of the story, but you are not the only part of the story. Everyone in your fellowship has skills and talents integral to the progression of your journey that you've never even dreamed of. Similarly, your grantees must be involved in the design phase of your measurement and reporting systems in order to feel ownership and accountability as you begin to implement this new approach.

Measuring and sharing your impact may also help you increase the giving that is the lifeblood of your operation. According to one study, 87 percent of charitable giving is produced by individual donors, and ***at least***

41 percent of these individual donors base their giving on an organization, funder, or agency's effectiveness and transparency.[5]

In summary, if you want to be effective, you must make data-based decisions on your social investments and then clearly communicate the effect of those decisions to individual donors, stakeholders, and the public. This means striving to achieve the greatest impact with existing resources (or even less). It means engaging in disciplined performance measurement and cross-sector collaboration to analyze the effect of your strategies on population outcomes. It means helping your grantees be the most effective they can be through guidance, regular communication, and standardized reporting processes. Ultimately, you will be helping to improve the relationship between funding and impact for all of us. One giant leap for humankind!

So how do we know if there is a return on social sector investments by our government agencies, foundations, and private donors? What systems, actions, and tactics will make it all possible? What evidence exists to support different approaches to measuring and improving social and public sector impact? Well, that's what my company Clear Impact has been working on figuring out over the past 15 years, and what I've condensed and laid out in the pages that follow.

Along with my colleagues at Clear Impact, I have learned a lot while establishing performance management and reporting systems for clients across the globe. Throughout this book, I'm going to share what I believe to be some of the most important aspects of implementing your own performance management and grantee reporting systems. Again, this will not be an exhaustive list of every step to be taken. I want this book to be easy to get through, immediately actionable, and I hope to make you smile in the process. That's why it's not overflowing with statistics and theories. That

5 https://www.fidelitycharitable.org/content/dam/fc-public/docs/insights/the-future-of-philanthropy.pdf

being said, I will mention additional frameworks, tools, and methodologies along the way that can help you do the nitty-gritty work when the time comes.

Generally speaking, it's better to start simple in this process. Breaking down our largest ambitions and goals into smaller, more digestible pieces will develop the necessary foundation to achieve sustained change. So, we'll start here with the basic overarching principles of an effective performance management system. Try to let go of your preoccupation with perfection along the way. As you learn and grow, your system may get more sophisticated, but you do not need to do everything perfectly from the beginning. Remember, an obsession with perfectionism is what breeds and propagates procrastination. Act now. And don't skip the action steps at the end of each chapter! Just get started and you'll be surprised at how much faster you'll progress on your journey to impact.

Throughout the following chapters, I'm going to provide you with a simplified system to help you get started, some stories to inspire your confidence, tools that can help, and a few action steps you can take to start implementing my recommendations as you read. I don't want you to be wary of "simplified." Simplifying our initial approach does not mean that this work is easy or that the social conditions we aim to change are simple. Again, small chunks. We are just breaking things down a bit so that we don't give up on our magnificent intentions.

Here's the system I'll guide you through:

1. How to create and align with a larger common agenda

2. How to sustain alignment with the common agenda

3. How to get started with Performance Measures in the simplest way possible

4. How and why to disaggregate your data for accurate analysis

5. How and why to develop the story behind your data for meaningful analysis

6. How to implement consistent and flexible grantmaking and reporting processes

7. How to use the data and corresponding story to initiate meaningful dialogue and action

8. How and why to share your performance data, action-plan, and reports publicly

Each chapter will contain two Social Sector Hero's Spotlights demonstrating how these steps have been implemented well or are in the process of being implemented. These will be government and philanthropic funder stories, but the processes and tips within are applicable to any public sector or nonprofit organization.

So, before we dive into the adventure that follows, I'd like to take a moment to commend you for taking action by opening up this book. Kudos on reaching the end of these early chapters! Celebrating each small step on our journey to change is an essential part of ingraining positive habits into your personal and professional lives. There will be ups and downs and that's inevitable. You will encounter giants on this path, and some may make progress seem impossible. Just remember, the most important step is the first one. Do what you can with what you have. You can reach measurable impact and you're doing it now by reading this book.

Let's get started!

CHAPTER 2:

REALIZE YOUR DESTINY
(ALIGN WITH A COMMON PURPOSE)

"The way a team plays as a whole determines its success. You may have the greatest bunch of individual stars in the world, but if they don't play together, the club won't be worth a dime." – Babe Ruth

Two of my sons play on a basketball team together, which I have the great joy of coaching. The team's goal in early 2022 was to win the championship, and we knew that if we were going to chart a course to that goal, we needed a way to measure our success. The metric we chose was to win a target number of games early on… and then we ended up losing three games in a month. If there was no championship agenda, the kids may have been OK with losing a few games. But they had all signed on to that Common Purpose, and the losses frustrated the heck out of them. The shared goal — and the lack of measurable progress — developed a hunger in them to take corrective action through practice and training. Sure enough, they worked hard at the process, and came back strong to win the championship.

I have been coaching youth sports for almost a decade and have played sports my whole life, and this is a pattern I've seen play out countless times.

The teams that work best together *always* have a Common Purpose or goal. Some teams are built for the championships from the get-go. For others, a successful season is winning one game. For some teams, it's simply ensuring that every kid feels included. Whatever the goal, there are always some constants: a clear destination (a Common Purpose), a game plan to reach that goal (a journey map), and the use of data to iterate towards success (reviews and analysis).

How does having a Common Purpose translate into better team performance? Well, once there's a clearly defined destination, you can create a journey map that includes all the data needed to get to your destination efficiently. The journey map outlines the biggest obstacles to progress and reveals the best way forward. When all the obstacles are outlined from the beginning, team members can plan viable actions and then assign those actions to the appropriate teammates. For example, an obstacle in basketball could be that an opposing teammate is particularly difficult to guard. Identifying the problem allows the team to identify appropriate solutions (such as selecting the team's best defender to guard the opposition).

Identifying a Common Purpose forces each player to view themselves as part of a whole. The point is not to be a team of individual superstars, but for everyone to maximize their strengths to create a powerful and cohesive unit that can't be beaten. Everyone can't be a three-point record breaker like Steph Curry. Some players can't make a three-point shot to save their life. But acknowledging your collective shortcomings and focusing on maximizing everybody's strengths gets the whole team closer to winning the battle. "Teams" of individuals focused on personal glory don't win championships.

Finally — and perhaps most importantly — a Common Purpose allows teams to measure their success. The measurement is what tells the team whether it's achieving the goal or not. It allows us to ask ourselves in real time: "Are we getting closer to our goal or farther away?" If you're on the right track, you can take a moment to encourage everybody's good work. If not, you can put an Action Plan in place to course-correct and get back on the path to success.

Reach Your Destiny Through A Common Purpose

Whether or not you enjoy sports or understand any of my basketball references, I hope it's clear that the same team-based approach works in the social sector — and in this analogy, you're the coach. Your organization and your funded partners must have a Common Purpose, consisting of a goal and an accompanying form of measurement, around which you design your journey map to social impact. Without this, your funded partners won't know where to focus their talents and resources. Everyone will be running in different directions, and there's bound to be collisions, duplications of effort, and a general sense of frustration.

Now, let's clarify what I mean by a Common Purpose.

There are two critical components to a Common Purpose and both are necessary if you hope to create alignment in your team's efforts.

Common Purpose = Result(s) + Indicator(s) that are shared among partners and utilized to guide all strategies and activities.

A Result By Any Other Name Would Smell as Sweet

First, you must have a tangible goal, vision, mission, outcome, result, destination... you get the picture. What you call it is not important — what matters is that you have one. I use the term "Result" to mean a condition of wellbeing that we want for our clients or communities. Results are big-picture goals, like: "Every child in our county possesses the skills necessary to achieve success in school and in life," or, "Every family in our neighborhood has access to healthy, unprocessed, fresh foods." Call it what you want, but you *must* have at least one, and you must ensure it's the same for the entire partnership.

A Result is:

1. The ultimate, big-picture outcome you desire for your community's wellbeing that you hope to achieve through your work and investments

2. Tangible enough that you can measure progress towards it

3. Shared among partners

4. Actively utilized to guide all strategy development.

When designing your Results, you're looking at an entire population of people, whether they participate in one of your affiliate programs or not. This is because ideally, we want all people to thrive. The hope is to reach as many of them as possible. So, your Results may often begin with "All..." or "Everyone..." Some funders have Results like, "All children enter school ready to learn," "All people are healthy," or "All families are economically self-sufficient." Not only do these consider whole populations, but they are also all measurable. The best Results are positive and aspirational in nature.

Are We Going in the Right Direction?

This brings us to the second part of a Common Purpose, and that's metrics, or Indicators. I define the term "Indicator" as a measure that quantifies the achievement of a Result. You must assign at least one Indicator to each of your Results. Metrics of all kinds can help you understand whether you're making progress towards your Results. If you don't have metrics, you really have no idea what's going on in your community. You'll have no idea if what you're doing is making any difference.

Now, some examples. Consider the Result, "All children in our county achieve success in school and life." There are many ways we could measure progress towards this social sector destiny. For example, you might want to monitor "Percentage of kindergarteners with age-appropriate development" or "Percentage of middle-schoolers enrolled in an extracurricular or after-school program" or "Percentage of twelfth-graders who report that they are exploring tertiary education or job opportunities."

Now, let's put it all together visually. Let's go back to that magical world where you found the scroll hidden behind the rock. Imagine you and your fellow travelers are looking at a map of a vast mythical land. Your village is suffering and facing a daunting enemy. You know the answer to your woes is out there somewhere, and you are itching to throw yourself into the adventures that await and desperate to help your community break free of its curse. Every adventure starts with just one step. But in which direction should you take that first step? You scan the map and it's full of winding rivers, steep mountainsides, deep valleys, and dark caverns. Suddenly, you notice the summit of a snowy mountain ridge. At the peak, it's labeled "Your village is peaceful, curse-free and all villagers are thriving." This is exactly what you were looking for — you just had to put it into words to really understand it! But how do you get there? Aha! You notice a path that leads almost directly to the mountain peak… though it's ridden with obstacles. How will you ensure you can stay the course? Your map's legend and your compass, of course! Now you have your clear destination, your method for measuring progress, and you can finally take that first step.

Here's what this journey might look like for funders. You might say, "Our **Common Purpose** is to ensure that **all children in our community enter school ready to learn** [your **Result**] by investing in shared strategies to improve the **percentage of kindergarteners with age-appropriate development** [your **Indicator**].

Of course, it's never as simple as this. You may have more than one Result, and it's common to develop multiple Indicators per Result. I recommend starting with no more than three Results and three Indicators per Result to help you get from talk to action quickly.

Hero's Journey Spotlight: Maryland Governor's Office of Crime Prevention, Youth, and Victim Services

In the mid-1990s, state governments across the USA began to unify their child-serving agencies. Lack of alignment among agencies manifested as a duplication of efforts, a lack of funding coordination, and poor communication. When this happens, service coordination is fickle, and too many children slip through the proverbial cracks. In Maryland, some Social Sector Heroes began converging to form their own fellowships — various partnerships, task forces, and offices aimed at improving service delivery to the State's children and families. And like any effective fellowship, they needed a Common Purpose.

To support the alignment that was already forming, Governor Parris Glendening created the Maryland Partnership for Children, Youth, and Families in May of 1998 (henceforth referred to as "the Partnership"). Glendening tasked the Partnership with devising a five-year State Plan for Children and Families that would illustrate how they would focus public and government attention on the needs of children, engage citizens in policy development, and distribute resources and funding in alignment with statewide goals for children and families.

In addition, the Partnership was tasked with guiding Maryland's agencies and 24 local jurisdictions (through Local Management Boards or LMBs) in implementing the five-year State Plan and producing the *Results for Child Wellbeing* publication. LMBs would identify community priorities and target resources for each jurisdiction. They would also serve as a coordinating entity and bring together local children's services agencies, local child providers, clients of services, families, and other community representatives to empower local stakeholders in addressing community needs and setting priorities.[6]

---

6 https://goc.maryland.gov/lmb/

How did the Partnership plan to create that public focus and alignment? Led by Chair Lt. Governor Kathleen Kennedy Townsend, they released their first budget priorities document in 1999 and announced eight Results (conditions of wellbeing for children and families) and 27 Indicators (measures to quantify the achievement of the Results). And bam! They had their Common Purpose. Today, the eight Results are:

- Babies Born Healthy

- Families are Economically Stable

- Children Enter School Ready to Learn

- Youth will Complete School

- Communities are Safe for Children, Youth, and Families

- Healthy Children

- Children are Successful in School

- Youth Have Opportunities for Employment or Career Readiness

You can access corresponding Indicators for each Result at SocialSectorHero.com/Resources.

Dr. Nancy Grasmick served as State Superintendent of top-ranked Maryland Public Schools for 20 years (starting in 1991) where she helped steer a fleet of 24 school districts comprising 1,424 schools and 869,113 students. Due to this vast leadership experience, Nancy was also invited to become a leader in the creation of the eight Results and 27 Indicators. Bonnie Kirkland, Special Secretary for the Office for Children, Youth, and Families in 1999 led the rollout of the Common Purpose. Arlene Lee joined the effort in 2005 when the partnership became part of the Governor's Office for Children and she gave it a reenergized focus with a "listening tour." The tour involved convening all child-serving advocates in connection with the National Governor's Association to reaffirm the value of Results and Indicators for children in Maryland. Countless local and state-wide leaders embraced the effort and coordinated resources for measurable change.

To this day, the Maryland Governor's Office for Children — now known as the Governor's Office of Crime Prevention, Youth, and Victim's Services (henceforth referred to as "the Office") — utilizes the eight Results for Child Wellbeing, now with 40 Indicators to guide and fund Maryland's 24 LMBs to implement planning for Children and Families. The Office promotes an overarching Common Purpose in addition to the eight Results, which is to "ensure all Maryland children, youth, and families live and prosper in healthy, safe, and thriving communities."

How did the Office aim to achieve alignment? To enact the Common Purpose through data-driven policies and collective solutions. As part of these data-driven policies, the Office now produces the *Results for Child Wellbeing* report in a digital format in Child Wellbeing Scorecards composed of data dashboards embedded on their website. You can learn more about these Scorecards broken down by jurisdiction at SocialSectorHero. com/resources.

The Office now spends around $16 million a year to fund initiatives serving children and families in the state. They also convene monthly meetings of Office staff and the Children's Cabinet — an agency entity that coordinates efforts to award funds to Maryland's 24 LMBs.

What was the impact of creating funding alignment through a Common Purpose for children and families? According to Arlene Lee, former Director of the Governor's Office for Children and chair of the Children's cabinet, school readiness improved from 49 percent to 83 percent in Maryland over a 10-year period. The 2013-2014 Maryland School Readiness Report reveals several other measurable improvements, including:

- 94 percent of African-American children were school-ready in 2013-2014, up from 57 percent in 2001-2002 and 91 percent in 2012-2013.

- The percentage of Hispanic children who were school-ready rose from 39 percent in 2001-2002 and 71 percent in 2012-2013 to 73 percent in 2013-2014.

- The percentage of children from low-income households who were fully school-ready rose from 34 percent in 2001-2002 and 76 percent in 2012-2013 to 77 percent in 2013-2014.

You can download the full report at SocialSectorHero.com/Resources.

How did they achieve such great success? Let's work backwards: Without the overarching guidance from the state's eight Results, particularly "Children Enter School Ready to Learn," there would be no coordinated effort to implement school readiness programming in the first place. The 24 LMBs may have been utilizing different Results or no Results at all. Without the Result, there would be no metric for kindergarten readiness. There would be no Results for Child Wellbeing Scorecard. The Results ensure the LMBs focus every action on improving the same Indicators and realizing the Common Purpose.

Be Brave and Lead the Charge!

You may be wondering who is responsible for setting the Common Purpose. Who should be involved? Should grantees have a say? What about the community? What about the donors? What about the local elected officials? In the interest of time and getting you started on your journey as fast as possible, I'm just going to come out and say it. You, as the funder and the backbone of the entire operation, are responsible. You must have the courage and confidence in your own expertise and capacity to set a clear path for everyone.

Why? You are the one spending thousands, hundreds of thousands, millions, and in some cases billions of dollars. Because of this, you have access to research, experts, tools, and other resources to guide everyone in the right direction. And according to Spiderman's Uncle Ben, "With great power comes great responsibility." You are a powerful force with a unique advantage. Use your force for the collective good and authentically hold yourself accountable for leading the charge. This will require courage and bravery, but I have complete faith that your belief in your mission will carry you through.

Your partners and grantees have joined you to form a fellowship with a Common Purpose. They are responsible for a large majority of the work. All partners in a fellowship need to have a common understanding of what they're working towards and a way to measure their progress towards the destination. This will allow each member to orient themselves in the same direction and recognize when they've strayed from the path.

Whether you're a government or philanthropic funder, the reason you exist in this role is to help accomplish something particular for the entire community through the power of social investment. You are the investor and you are the one with the most resources at your disposal, so feel secure in your authority to make the decisions around building a Common Purpose.

Your authority doesn't mean that you are the only Social Sector Hero, that you have all the answers, or that your funded partners or service recipients don't deserve a voice. Nothing would get done if this were the attitude. In fact, one study suggests that nearly 70 percent of people who are micromanaged report that it hurts their morale and more than 50 percent say it hurts productivity.[7] Grantee autonomy and community involvement in your strategy have an important place, particularly in individual

---

7 https://www.ajobthing.com/blog/autonomy-vs—micromanaging-which-is-better

organizational goal setting. This is where flexibility must work its way into the system.

Sometimes, you're not going to get it right. You may have to revise your Results and Indicators as time goes by. But every year you do it, you'll get better at it. And that's why it's OK for you to get started *right now*, right where you're at, with the resources you already have.

At this point in the process, I'm hoping you've considered what your social sector destiny might be and how you might be able to measure it. And I'll have some action items at the end of this chapter to help you brainstorm further. Now, you have to make sure everyone in your fellowship understands the Common Purpose and acts accordingly.

For the remainder of this chapter, I'll discuss some theoretical ideas on achieving alignment. In the next chapter, I'll help you put theory into action with specific steps. You cannot fulfill your Common Purpose without action. As Bilbo Baggins shouts enthusiastically in the theatrical version of *The Hobbit*, "We're going on an adventure!" Starting the adventure will force you to step out of the comfort zone of your Hobbit hole, but there's a whole world of impact waiting for you outside.

Understanding the Difference Between Common Purpose and Alignment

As I've said, a Common Purpose is the destiny you and your funded partners aim to realize, including a measurement strategy to keep you on the path. Alignment, on the other hand, is more about making sure that everything you do, individually and as a group, is in service of that destiny. You can only reach your destiny together with trust, healthy communication, and mutually supportive activities.

More specifically, alignment involves assigning appropriate roles and responsibilities to individuals within your social sector fellowship, keeping in mind the strengths, skills, and resources they bring to the mission. It's also about keeping watch over partners to ensure follow-through and to provide a helping hand when needed.

Alignment = You and all your funded partners:

1. Understand what the Common Purpose is

2. Understand what each individual's role is in achieving Results

3. Ensure every action you take is designed around the Common Purpose

4. Measure individual progress through program Performance Measures and consistently compare it to collective progress on community Indicators of wellbeing

5. Consistently communicate with each other to evaluate progress, identify common challenges, take corrective actions, and maintain momentum towards your destiny.

As a funder, how you make your social investments is really a function of how you envision your grantees aligning with your Common Purpose. The grant application process you design, therefore, can act as a first step towards creating an effective fellowship of Social Sector Heroes that actively align themselves with the Common Purpose. Your goal in the application process should be to find organizations that share your vision, have valuable knowledge and resources to share, are ready to engage in serious measurement, and commit themselves to collaboration despite any differences in opinion.

Want an easy test to see if you've already achieved alignment with your staff and grantees? Reach out to each funded partner and ask them to say, in one or two sentences, "This is what I understand the Common Purpose to be, here's my contribution to it, and here's how I measure that contribution."

Here's the kind of answer you're looking for: "We contribute to 'All babies are born healthy' and 'Reducing the percentage of low birthweight babies' in our community by providing low-cost prenatal services to women without insurance. To ensure we create measurable positive impact through these services, we measure and improve our 'Number of referrals of high-risk pregnancies to specialists' and the 'Infant survival rates' of our clients."

Consider The Theory of Aligned Contributions

On my personal journey to helping Social Sector Heroes achieve impact, I had the opportunity to work with Jolie Bain Pillsbury.

Jolie is the author of three books about Results-Based Facilitation, a cofounder of the Results-Based Facilitation Network and the Results-Based Leadership Consortium, and a founding co-director of the Results-Based Leadership Collaborative at the University of Maryland School of Public Policy.

With more than 30 years of experience as a public sector consultant and practitioner, Jolie developed the 'Theory of Aligned Contributions' in 2016. In it, she argues that large-scale population-level changes are more likely to occur when a core group of multisector leaders takes actions aligned towards specific common results.

Below, I will briefly lay out the elements of this theory and how they can help you achieve alignment with your funded partners. For more detailed information and instructions, you can find the full primer at SocialSectorHero.com/resources.

The Theory of Aligned Contributions defines the preconditions necessary to change social problems within the context of complex and adaptive systems. It utilizes thinking and terminology adapted from Results-Based Accountability and is built on the core assumptions that:

- Change must be multisector

- Unaligned action leads to unsatisfactory outcomes

- The intractable nature of social problems leads to a lack of urgency

- Public accountability can ignite urgency to solve problems

- A Common Purpose, relationships, and urgency leads to actions that create change

- Leaders must give themselves permission to engage in "action learning" (learning from actions and results as you go)

- Commitment to aligned action equips leaders to tackle difficult problems and adapt.

To create aligned action, organizations must ensure they meet the four following preconditions:

1. Focus on a Single, Measurable Population Result

This condition closely mirrors my recommendations on creating a Common Purpose with an important addition on populations, inspired by Results-Based Accountability.

First, identify the population you are intending to impact. Populations don't just include direct service recipients, but the entire target population that your services aim to help. Understanding this distinction will help you understand the difference between your community's wellbeing in its entirety and any change in conditions for the client population. The two are connected, but they must not be confused. Next, identify the desired conditions of wellbeing for the target population in plain language that anyone can understand. Next, determine measures that reveal whether the desired conditions of wellbeing are being achieved.

2. Urgency and Public Accountability

Make the information resulting from the steps in the previous condition publicly accessible and actively promote it to stakeholders, partners, and the community. The visibility of data is what leads to visceral and emotional reactions that ignite urgency to solve complex social problems. You and other leaders in your collaborative effort must commit to meeting regularly to analyze progress, course-correct, and remain accountable.

3. Leaders with a Collaborative Skillset

Develop the following competencies in key leaders:

1. Understanding the Results-Based Accountability 'Turn the Curve' process

2. Understanding how race, class, and culture underpin social conditions

3. The ability to host effective dialogues about race, class, and culture

4. The ability to take collaborative action

5. The ability to engage those you are accountable to in the development of strategy

4. The Four Quadrants of Aligned Contributions

Aligned actions translate into aligned contributions when individuals, organizations and communities within the collaborative system take actions that complement each other at a scale that is necessary to create change in the population. The degree to which leaders put effort into actions and their alignment with others results in a "quadrant" of alignment and action. All involved leaders should aim to reside in the "high action, high alignment" quadrant in order to have the best chance of success. The Theory of Aligned Actions becomes operational when enough leaders actively choose to engage in a high level of alignment and action — at the same time — to achieve measurable improvement.

Turn the Curve Thinking: The Ultimate Compass to Impact

There is one process that, when implemented in tandem across partners, can create more aligned action plans to improve all Community Indicators and Performance Measures, which we will discuss as we progress here. This process is called 'Turn the Curve Thinking' and is the central process of Results-Based Accountability. It is so effective that organizations around the world use it to maximize their impact, report on their funding, and communicate their efforts with stakeholders and the public.

Turning the Curve is about figuring out the steps we need to take today (the means) in order to reach our desired end state in the future (the ends). Specifically, turning a trend on a data graph from a negative or bad direction to a positive direction. Turning the Curve describes the efforts to improve the direction or rate of change in the baseline of an Indicator or Performance Measure. It is also a short-hand for the process of determining whether the current and projected level on an indicator or Performance Measure is acceptable or requires change.

I'm going to say this many times going forward, but that's only because it's so important — *less is more*. That's why I won't expect you to implement every single idea in this book all at once. It will be more effective for you to try one or two things and get really good at them than trying to tackle everything at once. So, if you only remember or want to implement one idea from this book — make it Turn the Curve Thinking. I believe it is the single most important tool to help you and your grantees realize your social sector destiny. If you utilize Turn the Curve Thinking as your common, repeatable, and scalable system for achieving social impact, all of the following conditions for success become possible:

1. Alignment across partners

2. A culture of continuous improvement

3. Accountability for action

4. Data-based decision-making

5. Data-based investing

6. Transparency and effective communication

I'll dive more deeply into Turn the Curve Thinking in future chapters.

Hero's Journey Spotlight: B'More Healthy Babies

On the east coast in Baltimore, Maryland there have been intentional efforts (and successes) to make measurable progress for children of color. In 2009, with deep racial divisions and a 61 percent African-American population, African-American babies in Baltimore City were five times more likely than white infants to die before their first birthdays. B'More for Healthy Babies (BHB) was created that year as an innovative initiative to reduce the infant mortality rate in Baltimore City through programs emphasizing policy change, service improvements, community mobilization, and behavior change.

The Baltimore City Health Department leads the initiative, with Family League of Baltimore and HealthCare Access Maryland serving as implementation partners. More than 100 corporate, nonprofit, academic, donor and government sector organizations participate as partner agencies. The initiative's strong community outreach and mobilization program operates in Upton/Druid Heights, Patterson Park, and other predominantly African-American neighborhoods. The BHB initiative works to decrease infant death in these communities by reducing the three leading causes: premature birth, low birthweight, and unsafe sleep. Their goal is to

"Improve an often-fragmented health care system to reach all of Baltimore's families with quality maternal and infant health services and support."[8]

Alignment with Maryland's "Babies Born Healthy" Result and corresponding Indicators like "Infant mortality rate" and "Black/white infant deaths" helped advance racial equity work and design efforts around making sure every child was born healthy in Baltimore. It also directly led to additional funding.

Among other efforts, BHB put alignment into action in the following ways:

- They worked to have all the city's birthing hospitals offer standard postpartum safe sleep education before discharge.

- They developed a centralized triage system to connect women to home-visiting programs and prenatal care.

- They worked with hospitals and health centers to offer a full range of contraceptive methods to all patients.

Since 2009, BHB has helped achieve the following results:[9]

- 35 percent reduction in the city's infant mortality rate

- 64 percent reduction in the disparity between black/white infant deaths

- 49 percent decrease in Baltimore City's teen birth rate

- 75 percent decrease in the black/white disparity in the teen birth rate

- 71 percent decrease in sleep-related infant deaths

---

8 https://health.baltimorecity.gov/maternal-and-child-health/bmore-healthy-babies

9 https://www.aecf.org/blog/using-collective-impact-to-reduce-infant-mortality-in-baltimore-city/

These measurable results attracted additional funders. Namely, the Annie E. Casey Foundation, based in Baltimore, MD, made major investments in both the City of Baltimore and State of Maryland's efforts. Local governments in Maryland's 24 local jurisdictions made additional investments.

The Annie E. Casey Foundation found the following to be critical lessons learned in sustaining a multisector collaboration in Baltimore:[10]

- No one entity — government agency, hospital, philanthropic organization, nonprofit, etc. — can do this work in isolation. Population-level change requires a partnership among residents and the private and public sectors. Developing these relationships takes time and may need organizations to realign their individual goals and priorities to support the initiative's overarching mission.

- Explicitly named and agreed-upon partnership principles can support authentic engagement and buy-in and shared decision making among partners.

- Family engagement efforts, including home visits, educational classes, and support groups, must be led by trusted community-based organizations and partners.

- Adopting an explicit focus on racial equity is critical. Addressing racial disparities in health or any other sector requires a deep understanding of underlying systemic and historical factors.

Judging by the two stories in this chapter, establishing a Common Purpose wasn't the only step required to achieve results for children in

---

10 https://www.aecf.org/resources/bmore-for-healthy-babies/#findings-and-stats

Maryland. Similarly, things won't just magically fall into place for your grantees after you communicate your goals and define your measures. But the lesson I want you to take from this chapter is that the Common Purpose (Results + Indicators) is what makes coordinated and effective action possible in the first place. Actions are more likely to lead to better results, more funding, and enhanced wellbeing for your community when they are all designed around the same goal. When every funded partner is laser-focused and aligned, amazing things happen.

CHAPTER 2 ACTION PLAN

1. Perform a simple test to see if your social impact fellowship is aligned:

   a. Email each of your funded partners and ask them to answer in two sentences maximum: "What are the Results we are all working towards, what is your organization's unique contribution to those Results, and how do you measure your individual progress?"

   b. Be sure to tell them that there are no wrong answers to the question. If you haven't made a concerted effort to communicate your vision, you can't expect them to know what the "right" answer is. Just be transparent and tell them their answer will inform efforts to create alignment for the group.

   c. Tell the grantee you will follow up at the conclusion of your experiment to either 1) affirm their answer, or 2) schedule a discussion around your Common Purpose and get their thoughts on how they align.

2. After completing Step 1, assess: were the answers from your grantees all over the place? If yes, bring together some key leaders in your organization and sit down for an hour to brainstorm and outline your Common Purpose with at least one Result and one Indicator. If not, audit your Results and

Indicators to make sure they align with the recommendations you discover as you work through this book.

3. Read the 'Theory of Aligned Actions' and the Results-Based Accountability Guide at SocialSectorHero.com/resources to enhance your understanding of the ideas discussed in this chapter.

CHAPTER 3:

SHEPHERDING THE FELLOWSHIP (ASSURING ALIGNMENT THROUGHOUT THE JOURNEY)

"Snowflakes are one of nature's most fragile things, but just look what they can do when they stick together."
– Vesta M. Kelly

A quick reminder before we dive into the practice of alignment:

Alignment is making sure that everything you do individually and as a group supports the achievement of your social sector destiny. It involves assigning roles and responsibilities to individuals within the fellowship that are appropriate for their strengths, skills, and resources. Creating your Common Purpose is only the beginning.

For some, the easiest way to understand why alignment is so important is to compare and contrast what things are like before and after any alignment efforts. I have a ton of first-hand experience here, as my company, Clear Impact, has gone through numerous transformations throughout the years that wouldn't have been successful without intentional effort around alignment.

In the early years at Clear Impact, the leadership team realized we needed to get serious about alignment to achieve our social impact mission. To do this, we enlisted key organizational leaders, staff, consultants, mentors, and methodologies (like Results-Based Accountability and the Entrepreneurial Operating System) to help us design a Common Purpose, enhance our focus, and clearly communicate this information to the company.

We then assisted each team in the development of departmental Performance Measures to monitor the impact of our actions against our company goals. Each team then assisted individual employees in the development of personal metrics to measure contributions towards departmental and, ultimately, company-wide goals. Every employee now has at least one metric they are responsible for tracking and improving.

When I asked some of our employees how they felt before and after the changes, one shared:

"There's a lot more structure now. I know what the goals are, including the measurable ones, so I know what to focus on. I can say, OK, what is the low-hanging fruit? What do I think is going to make the greatest impact first? Then, I just make sure that everything I do is in service of that measurable goal. Before, there was confusion because I didn't know where to start. I didn't really understand what my place in everything was, or how I was best suited to create impact. Without alignment, things took a lot longer than they needed to. Now that we have our goals and measures, I actually feel freer. There's no question about what needs to happen, so I am able to really get creative and apply my strengths in a more focused way. I can also tell immediately whether a new strategy is working or not. I also have a mechanism for justifying my department and its contributions, which makes me feel more secure and valued."

Alignment shows up everywhere. It's not just about actions. It also shows up in the hearts, minds, and emotions of the human beings that are on your social impact journey with you. When you can touch hearts and minds, you can generate more urgency, commitment, and enjoyment in the pursuit of your mission.

What Happens When There is No Alignment?

When there is no alignment, the partners in your fellowship may seem like they are running around like a bunch of chickens with their heads cut off, even though you know they have good intentions. Some team members, through no fault of their own, may have no idea what success even looks like, and will thus have difficulty meeting your standards and reporting requirements. Your funded partners may have completely different expectations of both you and fellow partners on the journey.

Lack of alignment can also generate negative emotions like confusion and apathy that impede progress even further. If people can't clearly see how they contribute to a larger shared destiny, action can seem futile.

In contrast, when you do achieve alignment, things look and feel very different from how they felt before. You'll see an enormous shift in communication, relationships, and the emotions felt by the individuals in you and your funded partners' organizations. Like I did with our Clear Impact employees, you can gauge this difference by simply asking your staff or partners, "Does anything feel different after we got serious about alignment?"

Hero's Journey Spotlight Part 1: U.S. Department of Education Promise Neighborhoods Program

In 2010, the U.S. Department of Education (henceforth referred to as "the Department") decided to create a new 'Promise Neighborhoods' Program. This decision was inspired by the successes of the Harlem

Children's Zone and the Promise Neighborhoods Institute based out of PolicyLink. From the start, Promise Neighborhoods were community-based initiatives meant to surround children in high-quality integrated programming designed around a multifaceted approach to healthy childhood development.

The Department's new Promise Neighborhoods program would begin providing three cycles of annual funding to support eligible non-profits, including faith-based organizations, higher education, and Native American Tribes and Organizations. Due to measurable improvements, Congress increased funding appropriation for the Promise Neighborhoods Program from $10 Million in 2010 to $73 Million in 2016.[11]

The Promise Neighborhoods program places high-quality schools, family involvement, and community engagement at the center of its work. Its mission is to ensure that "All children and youth growing up in Promise Neighborhoods have access to great schools and strong systems of family and community support that will prepare them to attain an excellent education and successfully transition to college and a career."[12] Social Sector Heroes involved in the program aim to achieve this mission through a complete transformation of communities, broken down by the following five areas:

1. Lifting up organizations focused on achieving results for children and families

2. Building 'cradle-to-career' solutions with great schools at the center

---

11 https://www.policylink.org/sites/default/files/PromiseNeighborhoods%20fact%20sheet%20February%202016%204.4.16.pdf

12 https://www2.ed.gov/programs/promiseneighborhoods/index.html

3. Breaking down silos and creating a support system for integrated programming

4. Developing local infrastructure and systems needed to scale efforts from the neighborhood level

5. Engaging in program evaluation to understand program impact and understand the relationship between program strategies and student outcomes.

The U.S. Department of Education created 15 Government Performance and Results Act (GPRA) measures — community Indicators of success that serve as a basis for how all Promise Neighborhoods report on their success. This is another real-world example of using Results and Indicators to orient a social impact journey.

You can view the full list of measures and other useful information about data at SocialSectorHero.com/Resources. I've abridged and shared five selected GPRA measures below to give you an idea of the program's multifaceted approach (e.g. health, neighborhood safety, educational outcomes, family involvement) and integration with childhood development, wellbeing, and success:

1. Number and percentage of three-year olds and children in kindergarten who demonstrate, at the beginning of the program or school year, age-appropriate functioning across the multiple domains of early learning

2. Number and percentage of children who participate in at least 60 minutes of moderate to vigorous physical activity daily

3. Number and percentage of students who feel safe at school and traveling to and from school, as measured by a school climate needs assessment

4. Number and percentage of parents (or family members) of birth to kindergarten entry-age children who read to their children three or more times a week

5. Number and percentage of students who have school and home access (and percentage of the day they have access) to broadband internet and a connected computing device.

Establishing GPRA metrics helped the Department of Education and all its funded Promise Neighborhoods align with a Common Purpose and create clarity around the purpose of the funding. But creating a list of measures is just the first step. Anyone can create a list of measures. To actually achieve measurable results for communities, funders must create a clearly defined and documented process for continual measurement, reporting, and strategy improvement. In other words, there needs to be a process designed to assure active alignment with goals and measures before, during, and after funding cycles.

The Department understood that sustained alignment and impact on child wellbeing would require a consistent reporting schedule and the use of program performance data to make investment decisions. So, upon piloting the program, they basically told each neighborhood, "We're going to invest up to $5 million in you… but we're also going to expect you to report annually on the 15 GPRA measures." By including program evaluation and impact reporting on measures designed around the five areas of community transformation, the Department could evaluate measurable returns on investments in each of the neighborhoods.

The Promise Neighborhoods program also understands the power of keeping score of their performance and allowing leaders to see what is going on in real time on the ground. This transparency in the data has created tremendous impacts on creating and maintaining aligned action. To sustain alignment with and passion for their mission, Promise Neighborhoods provides communities with a standard performance management system to report their data in the form of scorecards.

Due to aligned performance measurement, action, and accountability, many Promise Neighborhood communities are Turning the Curves on Indicators of wellbeing. Some of these, organized by community, include:

- Delta Health Alliance, Indianola Promise Neighborhood:
  - » Increased the four-year adjusted cohort high school graduation rate from 71 percent to 82 percent (2015–2021)

- Delta Health Alliance, Deer Creek Promise Neighborhood:
  - » Increased the four-year adjusted cohort high school graduation rate from 87.4 percent to 88.6 percent (2015–2020)

- Hayward Promise Neighborhood:
  - » Decreased the chronic absenteeism rate of students in sixth to ninth grade from 12.4 percent to 4 percent (2017–2022)
  - » Increased the percentage of kids who feel safe at school, and traveling to and from school from 60.4 percent to 77.7 percent (2019–2022)

- Berea College — Knox Promise Neighborhood:
  - » Decreased chronic absenteeism among sixth to ninth graders from 20.1 percent to 17.7 percent (2017–2019).

You can view graphs for these Turned Curves at SocialSectorHero.com/resources. In Part 2 of this Hero's Journey Spotlight towards the end of this chapter, we'll explore the story and Results of an additional Promise Neighborhoods funded community — the Mission Promise Neighborhood.

Your Journey Map to Alignment

So, how do you put all the theories and ideas about goals and alignment I've talked about into practice?

I've considered what our most successful clients have been up to over the past 15 years and refined the following five steps to help you create and maintain alignment in your organization and among your funded partners. It all starts with the creation of your Common Purpose.

Step One: Design your Common Purpose

Result = The ultimate outcome(s) of community wellbeing that you hope to achieve through your investments that are measurable, shared among partners, and actively utilized to guide strategy development.

Indicator = A metric that helps you determine whether your Results are being achieved.

Now is the time to define your collaborative's collective destiny. What do you want to achieve through your community investments? Ultimately, what are you hoping to achieve for your communities through the successful implementation of your grantees' funded programs? How can you describe these goals in the simplest terms possible?

Next, figure out how you're going to measure whether you're achieving your Common Purpose. This involves defining at least one Indicator for each Result. When you develop any metric, try to avoid analyzing more than one variable at a time. Do one thing at a time: trying to handle too many things at once will make measurement more difficult than it needs to be, and can cause confusion about the best path forward.

Remember, keep it simple at first. Define one Result and three Indicators that quantify the achievement of the goal.

Here are some examples of Results and corresponding Indicators:

Result: All babies in our community are born healthy

Indicator: Percentage of low birthweight babies

Result: All children are prepared to live successful lives

Indicator: High school graduation rate

Result: All people in our community are economically stable

Indicator: Percentage of people below 200% poverty

Step Two: Each Funded Partner Selects Relevant Performance Measures For Their Role.

A Performance Measure is a measure that answers any of the following three questions about a program or activity (first described in the Results-Based Accountability Framework):

1. How much did we do?

2. How well did we do it?

3. Is anyone or anything better off?

In the Performance Measure development process, make sure you ask each funded partner to create one measure that speaks to the *number served* (individuals, organizations, etc.). The most important type of Performance Measure, however, should speak to whether people are *better off* as a result of a program or service. These types of measures quantify the changes (or lack thereof) in attitudes, behavior, skills, knowledge, or life circumstances for service recipients. Ask your grantees to start measuring at least one Performance Measure per the two types (*number served* and *better off*).

I will provide more detailed information and instructions on Performance Measures in Chapter Four: Less is More.

Step Three: Implement a Unified Data Management System

Unified Data Management System = the same cloud-based software system utilized by all funded partners that standardizes, centralizes, and unifies data across funding streams to help you make better investment decisions.

Why does everyone need a unified data system like this? First, you'll never know what the latest version of your data is if it's kept in multiple places. Second, it's too difficult to build capacity across a system of partners if you don't have a common way of doing your reporting. Finally, it's impossible to make sense of performance data from different partners if they're all reporting in different ways.

The best Unified Data Management Systems will offer consistency, presentation, and ease of use. Ease of use is incredibly important; you don't want people to hate the system or they'll do everything in their power to avoid using it, and your progress will stall. It would be like trying to force everyone in your social sector fellowship to cross a river in boats riddled with holes. Finally, the system should allow you to tie the Action Plans to each respective measure. It should allow users to provide contextual information about strategies and actions as they relate to a specific measure so that you don't have to go searching for the actions you're looking for every time you have a question.

If you find a really superb system that you know will simplify data reporting for you and your partners, I would suggest making its use mandatory, rather than optional. Implementing a system will be a significant investment on your part, so why not get your money's worth and make it a condition of funding? Similarly, for partners that don't have data collection tools to support reporting, you may want to invest in data collection systems for them. To be clear, it is not important to have everyone using the same *data collection tools*. It is, however, important for them to be *reporting data* in a consistent way. Put yourself in the previous scenario: if someone in your social sector fellowship had a tool that was guaranteed to plug the holes in your boats so that you could all cross the river safely and efficiently, would you make it optional? Of course not! Just remember that if you choose to make any system mandatory, supporting partners through system training and capacity-building is a must.

There are lots of data management systems out there. Some will be better suited for your needs than others. For one example, consider checking out Clear Impact's data management systems at ClearImpact.com/software. Unification and alignment through data is our bread and butter.

Step Four: Host 1,1,1,1 (1x4) Meetings

Funders should sit down once a year for one hour to discuss progress on one metric with one grantee at a time (hence 1,1,1,1 or 1x4 for short).

Each hour-long conversation should consist of two parts. The first part should center around reviewing the Result and the Indicator that the grantee is contributing towards. During this discussion, you'll want to ensure that the grantee has a clear and comprehensive plan in place that you can get behind. What is their intended contribution and how exactly do they plan to make those contributions?

The second part of the conversation should involve a review of at least one of the grantee's Performance Measures. Since the next chapter focuses primarily on Performance Measures, I'll discuss how you and your grantees can use Turn the Curve Thinking to analyze your measures, determine an Action Plan, and report everything during the 1x4 meeting.

In short, your hour-long conversation will involve reviewing each of the following:

1. The state of the data

2. The analysis of the data (or the story the data is telling)

3. The partners who have a role to play in improving the data

4. Ideas to improve the data that have worked well for others

5. The resulting Action Plan

My best recommendation for holding these meetings effectively is to make them meaningful, concise, and time-bound. You don't want to add any unnecessary or stress-inducing meetings to anyone's day. This is especially relevant as some studies suggest that 67 percent of employees feel that spending too much time in meetings hinders them from being productive at work.[13] Whenever possible, you can incorporate these conversations into existing meetings to avoid adding more meetings to calendars. You probably have existing check-ins, and you can simply weave these conversations into those standing arrangements.

To be concise and time-bound, you should be able to cover both of these conversations in one hour. To make your meeting meaningful, you and your grantees should make sure you have an answer to the following question by the conclusion of the meeting: "What are the specific action steps that the grantee is going to take between now and the next reporting cycle and the next annual meeting?" This will give you something to start with at the next meeting. Many of these conversations will likely result in actions that you as a funder should take as well. Aim to serve your grantees from a supportive position rather than a punitive one in this process.

Step Five: Make Your Investment Decisions (Don't Fear Sacrifice)

Sacrifice is where change really happens. Sacrifice leads to growth. It can be extremely emotional, and it may be the hardest part of the Social Sector Hero's journey. This is because sacrifice represents the breaking of a pattern — patterns are comfortable, so often we hold onto them even when they're causing more harm than good. But patterns that aren't serving our values and mission must be broken.

Despite difficult reactions, Social Sector Heroes are willing to make sacrifices for the greater good. Sacrifice comes in many forms, but it is necessary to make progress on any mission. Just think about any superhero or adventure movie you've ever seen: the hero must always sacrifice something to reach the next stage in their journey. In the social sector realm, sacrifice may mean you must part ways with partners and/or programs that you feel an emotional attachment to. Sacrifice is hard but it will free up

---

13 https://otter.ai/blog/meeting-statistics

time, energy, and resources for the partners and programs that are achieving measurable impact in your community.

So, how do you decide where to make your investments and whether sacrifices must be made? Your 1x4 meetings with grantees should provide you with the data you need to make the best investment decisions possible. Use all the information at your disposal to invest in the partners and programs that have the greatest possible chance of maximizing your social impact and helping you achieve your purpose in the community. And *never* deny a grantee the opportunity to tell the story behind the data. Poor program performance in one year does not mean a program will never be successful. Just think about how the COVID-19 pandemic may have temporarily impacted the performance of the grantees who were working with you at that time.

One useful way to make decisions is to utilize a Performance Measure grading rubric that is customized to your organization. You can use grading rubrics during the grant application period, annual performance reviews, and the grant renewal process. You can score each Performance Measure review according to how well it adheres to the Turn the Curve Action Planning Process detailed in the next chapter. We've created a sample rubric that you can download for free at SocialSectorHero.com/Resources.

Don't Stray from the Hero's Path: How to Sustain Alignment Towards Your Social Sector Destiny

I'm sure you've heard it countless times: You need to have a Common Purpose and alignment to achieve success! What you may not have heard much about, however, is how to *sustain* that Common Purpose and alignment far into the future. Sustaining the alignment — or keeping your social sector fellowship together — is essential to staying the course and getting to your destination as quickly as possible.

The main way to sustain alignment around your Results is to make continuous improvement, measurement, and accountability an integral part of the organizational culture and systems you've designed. Additionally, be sure to encourage celebration upon achieving milestones (no matter how small they might seem).

But you don't have to take my word for it. Scientists and psychologists around the world have studied the positive impact that celebration can have on goal achievement. For example, researchers at Harvard Business School found that people who track small achievements every day enhance their motivation.[14] They also found that tracking progress releases dopamine in your brain, boosting mood, motivation, and attention. Dopamine also encourages you to keep doing activities that lead to the dopamine surge in the first place.

What does this all tell us? That tracking progress and celebrating successes can keep you and your funded partners engaged in the processes that you are tracking and celebrating for a longer period of time than if you just keep pressing on without ever acknowledging your progress.

Here are a few things you can do to maintain alignment towards your social impact through tracking and celebration:

1. Hold annual partner meetings.

The content can be up to you; what's important is maintaining consistency in the meetings and their agendas. You could consider doing any of the following as part of your meeting agenda: review progress on community measures of wellbeing, review the collective strategy, review progress on Performance Measures, and report on any key achievements.

---

14 https://extension.umn.edu/two-you-video-series/celebrate-small-stuff

2. Send out a monthly update to staff, funded partners, donors, and funders.

Updates can include any key areas of progress, highlights, or profiles of your Social Sector Hero of the Month — exemplary individuals demonstrating a commitment to your Results.

3. Host opportunities for free or reduced-price professional development opportunities or peer-led sessions for your staff and funded partners.

This could include hosting live workshops, offering virtual courses, facilitating skill-building sessions, or sponsoring certification courses. Your people will appreciate the support in their personal and professional development, and you can prioritize building internal capacity and skills that align with your Results.

Hero's Journey Spotlight Part 2: Mission Promise Neighborhood

In 2012, The Mission Economic Development Agency worked with the San Francisco Unified School District, the Office of Mayor Ed Lee, the John W. Gardner Center for Youth and Their Communities at Stanford University, United Way of the Bay Area, and various other partners from the Mission District to submit their proposal for a 'Mission Promise Neighborhood' to the Department of Education. In December 2012, they were selected to receive a Promise Neighborhoods Implementation grant.

As expected, Mission Promise Neighborhood (MPN) reported on the required 15 GPRA community indicators. MPN understood the importance of all the dimensions of child success that the 15 measures represented, but they felt that they could maximize their impact further by narrowing their focus. Based on community data, MPN found one of the most important GPRA measures to be the "Percentage of children entering school ready to learn," since studies showed that being ready for kindergarten is a predictor of third-grade, high school, and college proficiency.[15] This measure served as a "North Star" to guide the majority of their early learning efforts.

Focusing on ensuring children were entering school ready to learn led to many key discoveries, particularly when it came to school readiness and equity, that allowed MPN to focus their time, resources, and efforts on activities likely to accelerate change. In the 2018 to 2019 school year, MPN found that Latinx children in the Mission District were less likely to be school-ready at kindergarten than other children. The numbers showcased the disparity: the school-readiness average for schools in the Mission District was 48 percent overall, with White students at 65 percent, Black students at 50 percent, and Latinx students at 42 percent — the lowest percentage for all students in the report.

Revealing this disparity allowed MPN to design programs and strategies around impacting the children with the worst results first. They did this by providing children and families with "wraparound support" (engaging people who are already in the child's life to assess needs and develop more individualized support plans).

MPN employs a two-generation, whole-child approach in providing its children and families with wraparound support. They undertake high-quality and culturally responsive early care and education programs, along with broad family engagement and support. Partner organizations have developed strong relationships and refer families across the network to ensure they get all the services they need. MPN also emphasizes building parent leadership through its Abriendo Puertas/Opening Doors Leadership Program, since moms and dads serve as their child's first and most important teachers — and their best advocates. Abriendo Puertas/

---

15 https://missionpromise.org/si-se-puede-mission-promise-neighborhood-working-collectively-to-advance-racial-equity-by-improving-school-readiness-for-latinx-children/

Opening Doors has an evidence-based curriculum made by Latinx families for Latinx families.

Like the Department of Education, MPN realized that continued alignment would be a critical factor in its success. This would involve meeting with key players regularly and establishing a system for continual improvement and evaluation. This is why, early on, MPN began convening early learning partners to develop a shared agenda around school-readiness and to build targeted and aligned strategies. MPN continued to develop a strong network of partners that met regularly to share data, create shared measures, implement shared strategies, and figure out ways to engage families in culturally responsive and authentic ways. To support continued alignment, MPN utilizes Results-Based Accountability tools like the Turn the Curve Process to ensure data and strategy discussions translate into action.

So, what was the measurable impact of all this? A longitudinal cohort study implemented in 2018 demonstrated that four-year-olds whose families participated in MPN services had stronger scores in developmental assessments performed by teachers (across all domains of early-childhood success). Preschoolers who graduated from the MPN program and entered kindergarten in Mission District elementary schools were found to be 71 percent ready, compared to the wider Mission District average of 48 percent for that year. For Latinx children, the results were even higher, at 72 percent readiness. This means Latinx children in the Mission Promise Neighborhood outperformed the entire Mission District average by 24 percentage points.

In addition to its school readiness success, 80 percent of all Mission Latinx four-year old children are now in preschool. Since its inception, the Latinx high school graduation rate in the Mission district has also increased by 18 percent.[16]

MPN leadership — Liz Cortez (Associate Director) and Ada Freund (Early Learning Manager) — have noted the following three most important lessons learned around making their measurable progress for Latinx children:

1. Culture shift:

MPN partners work together to break down organizational silos, using a Collective Impact approach and RBA tools. This means working differently in various ways, running the gamut from developing a shared agenda for approaching school readiness to consistently sharing data.

2. Co-creation and capacity-building:

MPN partners have learned that it is most impactful to co-create with the community; in this case, with families of young children building their capacity to inform and lead this work.

3. Continuous improvement:

MPN partners are building a culture of continuous improvement that focuses on data review and strategy improvement. This requires constant adaptation based on community needs, such as those presented by the COVID-19 pandemic.

MPN's journey to success shows us that you really don't have to be "all things to all people" to experience growth and measurable success as a funder. The 15 GPRA Promise Neighborhoods metrics all represent critical areas of childhood development and success. But this doesn't mean

---

16 https://missionpromise.org/

that every single Promise Neighborhoods grantee has to focus on the same thing to achieve progress for children. Flexibility is also a big part of the equation for success. And without the flexibility to create their own focus, MPN may not have had the capacity to design their programming around lifting up Latinx children. MPN's story also shows us how a laser focus on Measurable Common Goals can be sustained through the creation of processes for strategy development, measurement, and continuous improvement (e.g. regular meetings to evaluate progress with key community partners).

CHAPTER 3 ACTION PLAN

1. If you haven't already done so, sit down with some key leaders in your organization to brainstorm one to three Results that you could use to guide your organization and funded partners. For each Result, define at least one Indicator that will quantify whether each Result is achieved.

    a. If you already have a list of goals and measures you're working with, audit the list. How many goals and measures do you have? Is each being actively used? Is there any way you could simplify or cut down the list?

    b. Make sure everyone in your organization and all of your partners have easy access to the list at all times.

2. Consider what it would take to start doing 1x4 meetings with each of your funded partners. Create a list of the actions that would need to happen to make these meetings effective. What information would you need? What tools and processes would need to be put into place? Would a Unified Data Management System be helpful?

3. If a Unified Data Management System *would* be useful, start exploring what's available. Clear Impact software systems are just one option available to you. You can learn more at https://ClearImpact.com/software if you are interested in exploring these systems.

CHAPTER 4:
MINIMIZE SIDE-QUESTS (REMEMBER, LESS IS MORE)

"The successful warrior is the average man, with laser-like focus."
– Bruce Lee

I have four kids, and one of the things I've learned on my parenting journey is that *less is more* — especially when it comes to holidays. While my wife may disagree, I believe that when we buy too many gifts, the attention spent on each dwindles more rapidly than when there are fewer gifts. Because I love data so much, we could look at this mathematically and say that X (the number of gifts purchased) is negatively correlated with Y (the perceived value of each gift).

Sometimes, the kids will start playing with the boxes and completely forget about what was in them! I'll have one running around the house with a box on his head and another one trying to ride down the steps into the basement. It gives me a lot to laugh about, and I love that they're being creative, but talk about being distracted by the wrong things! After a month, the toys are at the bottom of the toy pile, completely forgotten (and the now-shredded boxes have been discarded too).

I have found that buying fewer, more valuable gifts is the way to go. By giving each kid a handful of presents that they really want, they play with them for longer. Everyone is happier, there's less waste, and the house is less cluttered. My wife and I are also either 1) saving money or 2) spending the same amount of money, but only on things that get used.

Now, let's pretend your "presents" are the various activities you and your funded partners engage in. So, presents can be projects, programs, Indicators, Performance Measures, strategies, meetings, processes… the list goes on and on. You can apply my gift-giving principle to your own work. When it comes to realizing your social impact destiny and creating measurable impact, *less is more*.

Side-Quest = an extraneous activity or detail that distracts you from the mission at hand or has little to no value.

When you minimize the number of "side-quests" you embark on, you'll be able to focus on the most important journey of all — achieving a positive impact in your community. Like my kids, when you give yourself too much to do and jump from 'toy' to 'toy', you'll have less time and resources to spend on each individual project. You'll find that some projects may be abandoned entirely, resulting in frustration and wasted resources.

To help you remain focused on the most important tasks at hand, I'm going to practice what I preach and center this chapter's lesson around two main ideas:

1. How to develop Performance Measures
2. How to implement a simple, repeatable system to guide everything you do

Avoiding Data Overload

I'm fully aware that this chapter may be the most psychologically difficult to implement. When you're as driven as a Social Sector Hero, it may seem like you should consider every piece of data or unit of information available. But the opposite is true — data overload can lead to what some of us in the industry refer to as "analysis paralysis."

While I appreciate our unprecedented access to data and information, it's not always positive. In 2016, Pew Research Center (PRC) found that when public sector institutions expect their partners to use too much information to perform tasks, many partners feel too burdened to do their jobs effectively.[17] Additionally, 46 percent of Americans agreed with the following: "A lot of institutions I deal with — schools, banks or government agencies — expect me to do too much information-gathering in order to deal with them." Furthermore, those who agree are 26 percent more likely to experience elevated levels of stress.

Just think about it. Say you expect your grantees to report 20 Performance Measures and you have 20 funded programs. This means you have 400 Performance Measures to evaluate. It doesn't sound fun, does it? And if your grantees aren't reporting on similar or identical measures, the problem is exacerbated. The more measures, the less time you'll all be able to spend on each, and the less you'll be able to improve performance as a whole. And that's simply not fair to you, your grantees, or the communities you serve.

So how can you ensure you come to work each day with a deep focus on what matters most? By the time you reach the end of this chapter, I'm hoping you'll agree that when setting up your performance management system, you really don't need more than three to five Performance Measures per focus area (however you define that) to understand your shared impact. Fewer measures lead to greater efficiency and less stress. Performance measurement should be a means to an end — not a compliance exercise.

---

17 https://www.pewresearch.org/internet/2016/12/07/information-overload/

From Alignment to Performance Measurement

In the last couple of chapters, I asserted that the primary condition of alignment is creating and sustaining a Common Purpose (ie, Results and Indicators). A huge part of sustaining alignment is also providing partners with a Unified Data Management System to report Performance Measure data and program progress. Now, my job is to help you help your grantees design Performance Measures that keep you focused. The methods I present will act as a journey map to guide you along the path to social impact.

The biggest side-quest time-wasters involve 1) requiring too many Performance Measures and/or 2) focusing on Performance Measures that don't reflect the programmatic impact on clients or communities.

The most important Performance Measures your grantees should focus on answer one simple question: Is anyone better off as a result of our service? Or, what were the changes (or lack thereof) in attitudes, behaviors, skills, knowledge, or circumstances? Other kinds of measures — like the number of clients a program serves or the number of program pamphlets handed out — can be useful, but they shouldn't be a proxy for impact.

To maintain alignment, every funded partner should report on a maximum of five metrics. The metrics should primarily speak to the role that the organization plays in achieving the Common Purpose. Why five? Any more than that and the action becomes unfocused, the resources are spread too thin, and burnout will spread. Exercising restraint will ensure urgency and accelerate progress towards the social impact destiny.

Designing Performance Measures

What are Performance Measures?

Performance Measure = a measure that does one of three things: 1) quantifies activities associated with a program or initiative, 2) speaks to the quality of that initiative, or 3) speaks to the effect of the initiative on the client population.

Some of the information in this section will be a recap, but there are a few more things to consider. I would like to provide you with some examples of effective Performance Measures and speak to an obstacle that emerges when comparing Performance Measures across funding streams, programs, and grantees.

The Three Types of Performance Measures

The Results-Based Accountability framework presents three questions any program can ask to design Performance Measures. I will present the three questions below and utilize a fictional after-school reading program to serve as an example:

1. How much did we do?

- Number of program participants (number of total children enrolled in the ABC After-school Reading Program during the 2021/2022 school year)

- Number of program actions (number of successful reading sessions held)

- Number of goods distributed (number of informational brochures distributed to parents)

2. How well did we do it?

- Program attendance rate (average attendance rate for each reading session)

- Participant satisfaction (average percentage of kids who said they had fun at the conclusion of each guided reading session)

- Percentage of staff with training/certification (percentage of program coordinators with formal teaching or early childhood development credentials)

- Cost/benefit ratio (ratio of average dollars spent per child participant compared to percentage of children with improved reading scores after X months)

3. Is anyone or anything better off?

- Number/percentage of participants with improved attitudes (percentage of parents who reported that their child has increased interest in reading after program completion)

- Number/percentage of improved participants with improved knowledge (percentage of children who improved reading scores after X months)

- Number/percentage of participants with improved behaviors (percentage of children that read outside of school at least once a week)

Selecting Performance Measures

There are two fundamental ways you can instill Performance Measures for your grantees:

1. If your funded partners are implementing the same or similar programs, you can develop a standard set of Performance Measures across like programs.

2. You can let each grantee choose Performance Measures for themselves.

You will probably want to engage in some combination of the two approaches above. The most important thing is that there are common performance management and reporting systems in place. The systems must be flexible enough to account for differences among grantees. Grantees must be able to talk about their stories and explain unique circumstances.

At the very least, provide them with guidance on what an ideal Performance Measure looks like, using the three questions above.

In the Performance Measure development process, make sure you ask each funded partner to create at least one measure that speaks to the *number served*. The most important type of Performance Measure, however, should speak to whether people are *better off* as a direct result of the program or service being implemented. These types of measures quantify changes (or lack thereof) in attitudes, behavior, skills, knowledge, or life circumstances for service recipients. Ask your grantees to start measuring at least one Performance Measure per the two types (*number served* and *better off*). Grantees should always be engaged in choosing their Performance Measures, so that they 'own' them and really want to use them.

Again, in total, you only need three to five measures to effectively assess a program.

You can access more detailed instructions on creating Performance Measures at https://SocialSectorHero.com/resources.

Hero's Journey Spotlight: United Way Worldwide

United Way (UW) is a global, diverse network of over 1,100 local nonprofits serving communities 42 countries.[18] With $5.2 billion in revenue reported in 2021, it is the largest charitable organization in the United States. It is also the largest nonprofit organization as measured by public donations. UW's main purpose is driving community change to help people to live good lives, most often by working to ensure that everyone has access to a quality education, economic opportunity, and the ability to live healthy lives. Each United Way is independent, with its own donors, partners, and funded agencies.

---

18 https://en.wikipedia.org/wiki/Nonprofit_organization

In 2015, Social Sector Heroes at United Way Worldwide realized they needed a common measurement framework for every UW affiliate to report on to document the Network's collective reach and impact. This led them to develop the Global Results Framework (GRF) — a set of core reach and outcome indicators in key impact areas used to report progress. Impact areas include Childhood Success, Youth Success, Economic Mobility, Access to Health, and Community Engagement. The GRF is designed to demonstrate social impact, highlight shared strategies and approaches across the United Way Network, and motivate potential donors to give. To accomplish this, the GRF aggregates results across United Way communities to accomplish four main goals:[19]

1. Demonstrate shared return on social investment

2. Simplify and align results

3. Convey the scale of impact across markets and geographic locations

4. Create a compelling story and narrative to drive action

What prompted these efforts? This is only part of the story, but national partners and multinational corporations communicated a desire to understand why they should invest in the entire United Way network, rather than donating directly to nonprofits funded by UW. The fundraising landscape is hyper-competitive and it has become easier for nonprofits to fundraise directly from corporations. To convince investors of the network's value, UW used aggregated GRF results to demonstrate how they were uniquely positioned to leverage necessary resources for change and maximize the potential for impact on shared priorities across funded partners and local United Ways.

---

19 https://www.uwp.org/wp-content/uploads/GRF-PA-Slides.pdf

I got involved with UW in 2017 when Evan Hochberg (former Chief Strategy Officer at United Way Worldwide) spearheaded the search for a performance management platform that supported the UW and GRF's purpose and mission. Part of Evan's big strategic plan was to strengthen and maximize UW's relevancy for fundraising. There were a few other Social Sector Heroes who got involved too: Alicia Lara, former Senior Vice President of Impact, Ayeola Fortune, former Senior Director of Impact and Global Results, and Jeff Elder, former Director of Social and Economic Research (all at UWW).

The first time I met with Alicia, Ayeola, and Jeff, they came to the table with a list of more than 80 measures for affiliates to report on after working with a prior consultant. And I get why the first list was long — United Way's hyper local approach enables the Network to serve thousands of unique communities with varying needs. Similar circumstances usually prompt funders to develop an absurd number of measures. However, UW understood that this was way too many measures for their Network to report on, and they cut many of them throughout a series of discussions internally and with their Network. Their new challenge was to create indicators that were high-level and could simultaneously reflect the diversity of strategies, approaches, and strategic investments.

There are two main ways UW utilized the 'less is more' mentality to simplify participation in the new GRF and performance management systems. First, after much discussion and emphasizing the value of 'less is more', we cut the list of 80 down to 48 measures, with an average of 12 measures per UW result focus area:

1. Childhood Success

2. Youth Success

3. Economic Mobility

4. Access to Health

5. Community Engagement

Secondly, UW made it even easier for affiliates to get started by allowing them to opt-in to the action areas where they did their best work. To make performance reporting more manageable, United Ways were allowed to pick a minimum of one measure in any of the four impact areas to report on. While some larger United Ways could report on more, it was important to support every United Way that wanted to participate. All this simplification lowered barriers to entry and made it more feasible for even small United Ways to participate in the GRF.

Alicia once referred to this project as "UWW's moonshot" to maintain relevance in their fundraising efforts. The GRF allowed UWW to run reports of impact by geographic region that were important to certain corporate donors in order to maintain their competitive advantage. The result? United Way had already amassed an impressive list of corporate sponsors prior to the GRF efforts, however, the GRF helped shore up UW's value proposition related to several companies' longterm investments.

United Way has amassed an impressive list of around 200 corporate sponsors over the years, across an array of industries, including American Express, Amazon Smile, Starbucks, Wells Fargo, Microsoft, the National Football League (NFL) Foundation, and many more.[20]

Ayeola's proudest moment was in 2020 when, four years into the GRF, there was buy-in and support across UWW internally and across the entire network of individual UWs. The GRF was now operationally institutionalized. Everyone could see that the GRF produced tangible and measurable outcomes that UWW could bring to fundraising conversations with corporate partners. These were things like, "7.1 million people accessed healthy food and physical activity" and "billions in tax returns generated." A few corporate partners were so convinced that they began asking for advice on how to do performance measurement! Unfortunately,

---

20 https://www.unitedway.org/our-partners

due to extenuating circumstances, UWW had to pause data collection in 2021, but this doesn't detract from prior measurable results.

United Way Worldwide also provides public access to its aggregated impact data across the four focus areas: access to health, childhood success, youth success, and economic mobility, as well as community engagement, in the form of "Global Snapshot" reports every year. These snapshots share notable measurable improvements, in addition to individual success stories to add a human touch. Based on the 2020 snapshots, we can see that the United Way has worked with community partners to deliver the following community results:

- 81 percent of children and adults served ate healthier, increased physical activity, or moved towards a healthier weight
- 678,569 community residents participated in meetings
- 85 percent of children maintained or improved school attendance
- 40 percent of individuals increased their wages
- 97 percent of youth transitioned from middle to high school on time

You can access the full Global Snapshots and Indicator data at SocialSectorHero.com/Resources.

Want to take a similar initiative in your organization to drive donations and obtain more sponsors to develop your own compelling impact snapshots? Ayeola shared the following tips to help you get started — many of which mirror the lessons we've explored in this book so far:

- Be ready to invest in training and capacity-building, particularly for performance management, at least once per year
- Start small and be sure to do something with every measure

- Be consistent and avoid changing your measures to maintain buy-in and support

- Co-creation in performance measurement will give your processes legitimacy

- Help people support continuous improvement locally — engage regularly with grantees

- Have a developmental mindset. Learn as you go. Consider what worked and what didn't

- Think about sustainability in your staffing, coordination, tools, and resources

What do I want you to remember from the legend of United Way? 'Less is more' thinking generates more buy-in because it makes things less burdensome and more meaningful to your funded partners. Use fewer measures! Even after reducing the data burden and simplifying GRF participation requirements, UW was able to make the case for a larger potential impact. It's not about getting rid of everything you're doing — it's about enhancing value through minimalism.

This is where things start to get really exciting, because it's where Turn The Curve Thinking really comes into play.

'Turn The Curve' Meets 'Less Is More'

Earlier I mentioned Turn the Curve Thinking: that critical process of turning a negative data trend around into a positive one. How does Turn the Curve Thinking align with less is more thinking? Well, when you use this process to guide every data-related decision you make, you reduce the number of processes you must learn, practice, implement, and evaluate. When you ask your grantees to use it in grant applications, performance reporting, and grant renewals, you can more easily evaluate the impact of your investments — you already know the process and framework!

Once your grantees determine their Performance Measures (or you determine your Community Indicators), everyone should continually engage in the Turn the Curve Thinking Process to monitor and improve each metric. The process consists of the following steps:

1. Graph the chosen measure including a history and a data forecast (where the data is headed if you do nothing differently).

This is where the use of a Unified Data Management System comes in handy. Manual graph creation, custom data calculations, data accuracy, forecasting, and data analysis are tricky if you don't have a degree in data analysis. Even if you do, the tasks are still time-consuming. Data management software is a godsend that will automate some of the most time-consuming tasks, ensure more accuracy and security of your sensitive data, and centralize your data from funded partners for easier organization and analysis.

2. Explore the Story Behind the Curve (the contributing and limiting factors).

This step requires you to analyze the multitude of factors that contribute to the data history, trendline, and forecast. When completing this step, think about all the obstacles that prevented this measure from improving in the past. Or, think about all the positive things that happened that may have contributed to an improvement. If you are experiencing particularly difficult times and/or extenuating circumstances, think about what may have prevented the data from being worse than it is. Here, it is important to dig deeper than you ever have before as you work to identify root causes.

3. Identify new and existing partners who have a role to play in changing the data.

This one is pretty straightforward. There are a lot of players in the game of Performance Improvement. Think about all the staff involved in delivering the program. Think about all the community partners who influence the successful delivery of the program. Who is helping you? For example, partners for an after-school reading program might include parents, local school districts, libraries, education-focused nonprofits in the community, local government agencies, and obviously the children themselves. Think about what you might need from each partner in order to run a successful program. Also think about some non-traditional partners you can engage to support your efforts.

4. Brainstorm What Works to improve (ideas may include low-cost options, actions proven to work in other communities, or new ideas with high potential).

Start brainstorming what might work to address the Story Behind the Curve and improve the Performance Measures. There are a few different types of "What Works" ideas that you should consider. When you're getting started, try not to be too restrictive. You can always pare down the list later, but you may miss out on some innovative ideas if you restrict answers. Consider the following:

1. Ideas that have worked for other communities
2. Ideas that have worked in the past in your community
3. Ideas that are supported by evidence
4. Ideas that may not have been implemented but seem like they would have a good chance of working
5. Ideas that might seem outrageous or unorthodox
6. Ideas that might cost too much but are likely to work
7. Ideas that would be cheap or have no cost at all.

5. Narrow down your ideas on what works to create an Action Plan.

When you've generated a sufficient number of ideas, you can narrow down your list into priority ideas that are likely to Turn the Curve (improve the data baseline) on whatever measure you're looking at.

For real change to happen, you must then transform your priority ideas generated in Step 4 into an Action Plan. Determining the Action Plan will involve assessing the appropriateness of each action according to four criteria: leverage, feasibility, specificity, and values. You can assess an action's appropriateness by exploring the following four questions for each criterion:

1. Leverage: How strongly will the proposed strategy impact progress as measured by the baselines?

2. Feasibility: Is the proposed strategy feasible (technically, politically, financially)?

3. Specificity: Do you know who, what, when, why, and how?

4. Values: Is the strategy consistent with the values of your organization, community, etc.?

You can learn more about the four criteria for selecting actions in the RBA Guide, accessible at SocialSectorHero.com/resources.

Each Action Plan should include the steps involved, who will be responsible for completing each step, and a timeline. In addition to due dates, the timeline should give a bird's eye view of the scope of the entire project. Design the Action Plan with accountability in mind. Software systems are also useful here if they provide a mechanism for tracking progress (e.g. a progress bar, Gantt Chart, or checklist).

Turn the Curve Thinking is not a set-and-forget process. Rather, it is iterative or circular. That means that whenever you reach the last step, you should go through the entire process again at regular intervals. If you choose to utilize the 1x4 meeting schedule from the last chapter, the interval would be once per year. These conversations should be about revisiting what was discussed before, identifying new factors, revisiting Action Plans, etc.

If you want a quick overview of some of these efforts, take a look at the Clear Impact website case studies page. We also have a large list of Turn the Curve Action Plans specifically related to racial equity efforts from our 2021 Turn the Curve Action Plan Poster Contest. You can access both of these resources at SocialSectorHero.com/Resources.

Examples of Side-Quests to Avoid

Hopefully I've convinced you of two things: 1) don't ask your grantees to report on too many Performance Measures and 2) Turn the Curve Thinking is indispensable. When you get started on your journey to social impact, there are a few other side-quests you should avoid:

1. Spending hours creating or discussing Turn the Curve Action Plans.

In my experience, most leaders possess enough background knowledge about what's going on in their field. You can do Turn the Curve Action Planning in an hour or less. I've seen people spend hours or days on each step, and this can lead to a bunch of questions, conflicts, objections, and distractions. Remember, you can always come back to the plan later. Don't get caught up by perfectionism.

2. Creating too many Results or Indicators.

Try to limit your number of Results to no more than three to five. The same goes for Indicators. Three to five Indicators for each Result will prevent you from losing focus on the most important factors impacting community wellbeing.

3. Requiring grantees to report on Performance Measures without providing a standard mechanism for doing so.

If you desire timely, consistent, and actionable data, you must provide your social sector fellowship with a standard performance reporting system and/or tools. Your partners need an easy way to capture and report on their data. Without consistent reporting systems and tools, collecting data from grantees can feel like herding cats.

Less is More in Grant Applications

Less is more shows up in much more than Performance Measures and Turn the Curve Action Plans. In my experience, one area in which the mindset has yet to be applied across the board is the grant application process.

Grant applications are usually onerous. They ask too many questions and often the questions are redundant. What should you do differently? Try to make the grant application process as easy as possible. This may include allowing organizations to utilize the same metrics they're using for other grants. It could also mean utilizing a grant application and performance reporting software that's the same for every grantee. When designing your grant applications, you should focus on four main pieces of information:

1. What the organization does

2. The intended outcomes they aim to achieve through the grant

3. How they plan to achieve those outcomes

4. How they plan to measure progress.

The same goes for grant renewals and requests for additional funding. For these processes, ask your grantees to report on key measures and provide a brief Turn the Curve Action Plan for each. You'll want to understand the current state of the data, significant areas of progress, any obstacles to improvement, and changes to Action Plans.

I envision different funders in different locations utilizing the same frameworks and tools to measure social impact. This would make reporting much easier for any given grantee receiving multiple grants from different funders. Just imagine what would happen if all funders in a country, state, or neighborhood utilized Turn the Curve Thinking to measure community wellbeing and program impact.

What can you do as an individual funder to make these wild dreams come true? Consider taking the initiative to call on fellow Social Sector Heroes to convene and explore the benefits a common approach to impact and performance measurement can deliver. Frame the conversation around how alignment will accelerate improvement in the wellbeing of children, adults, and families in your community. It doesn't matter if you talk about the specific ideas or frameworks in this book — just keep the focus around what you hope to collectively achieve and how you can make it happen faster through alignment of action.

Hero's Journey Spotlight: Baltimore City and OutcomeStat

Andrew Kleine is currently Senior Director of Government and Public Sector at the global advisory firm EY-Parthenon. As his LinkedIn profile says, he truly is "Good Government Guy." Without his efforts, Baltimore City's OutcomeStat initiative may be a figment of our imagination.

Andrew joined the City of Baltimore in 2008 as the Budget Director. He spent a decade in this position during a tumultuous time of political scandal, economic crisis, and civil unrest. Andrew found his own wizard of sorts in his quest for good government in Baltimore: in *The Price of Government*, David Osborne and Peter Hutchinson describe a common-sense approach to "squeezing more value out of every tax dollar" called Budgeting for Outcomes. The book — or journey map if you will — inspired Andrew to bring what he called Outcome Budgeting and, ultimately, OutcomeStat to Baltimore. Outcome Budgeting makes outcomes the starting point for budgeting — instead of last year's spending plan. Budgeting becomes about funding outcomes instead of organizational units. It's about using data and evidence to make budget decisions. For example, an agency engaging in Outcomes Budgeting will reward programs that get measurable results and repurpose dollars from programs that don't.

The OutcomeStat initiative grew out of a desire to integrate Baltimore's strategic planning, budgeting, and performance management processes, which were largely siloed and uncoordinated. Andrew tells a detailed story about OutcomeStat in *City on the Line: How Baltimore Transformed Its Budget to Beat the Great Recession and Deliver Outcomes*. While learning more about OutcomeStat could be useful to you, it is not the focus of this chapter, so I point you to his book to learn more (forgive me for the side-quest). When you do get your copy, check out Table 1.1 on page 12 for a summary of the changes in Baltimore's budgeting process.

To initiate OutcomeStat, Andrew took the 'less is more' philosophy to heart. This mindset aided the creation of the city's Common Purpose (labeled Priority Outcomes) and accompanying measures of success (Key Indicators). The City established seven Priority Outcomes with an average of three Key Indicators for each (see Table 1 below, adapted from "Baltimore City OutcomeStat Indicators").[21] With Outcome Budgeting in mind, Andrew's guiding principle for the City's budget was to "purchase" measurable improvements for each Priority Outcome and Key Indicator. As a result, funds were allocated to Outcomes — not agencies.

---

21 https://bbmr.baltimorecity.gov/sites/default/files/outcomes%20and%20indicators.PNG

Let's look at some examples:

Priority Outcome	Key Indicators
Better Schools	• A safe and healthy start • Kindergarten readiness • Academic achievement • College and career readiness
Safer Streets Stronger Neighborhoods	• Shootings • Property crime • Citizen perception of safety • Blight elimination • Neighborhood investment • Sustainable transportation • Recreation visits
A Healthier City	• Heroin-related deaths • Citizen mental health • Childhood asthma
A Growing Economy Innovative Government	• City resident employment • Jobs in Baltimore • Visitors to Baltimore • Lean government • Innovation fund
A Cleaner City	• Recycling rate • Citizen perception of cleanliness • Cleanliness of waterways • Energy usage

An important innovation of OutcomeStat was to bring together more than 200 partners from inside and outside of city government to develop Turn the Curve plans for each Key Indicator. For the first time, the

City had a single set of consensus plans to guide agency budget proposals and the Mayor's budget decisions.

To create buy-in and align city management, Andrew required each of the city's 250 services to report exactly five Performance Measures each. This approach to performance reporting continues to this day under the leadership of Budget Director Bob Cenname. Revisiting the tip on succession from the previous Hero's Journey Spotlight, you should "think about sustainability in your staffing, coordination, tools, and resources." Bob was Andrew's deputy for seven years, so the buy-in was already there. This created continuity in the budgeting journey.

Ultimately, the sustainability of the collective effort rests largely on the 'less is more' approach from the beginning. If the City had requested double or triple the measures from funded services (10 or 15 as opposed to five), the services may have revolted as they have in so many other contexts and locations. Performance reporting would have been far too time-consuming and less useful. Progress may have stalled or broken down completely.

To get agencies even more focused on the most critical results, Andrew asked them to build Turn the Curve Plans for one outcome-oriented performance measure per service. This step was supported by Clear Impact's Scorecard software platform, which was adopted by Baltimore's CitiStat performance monitoring program. Until OutcomeStat, CitiStat had been stubbornly low-tech, relying on spreadsheets to track data.

As we saw in the United Way journey, fewer measures do not mean fewer measurable results or anecdotal successes. I implore you to let go of that notion! Here is just a sampling of the City's results:

- Investing in home-visiting and other services led to a drop in the infant mortality rate from 13.5 to 8.4 deaths of children less than one year old per 1,000 live births from 2009 to

2015, even as the City struggled with the fallout of the Great Recession.

- Baltimore allowed agencies to propose service takeovers from other agencies if they could prove more efficient delivery of the service. One result was that the Mayor's Office of Human Services took over the management of child care centers from the Housing Department and provided summer learning loss programming to 1,100 additional children at no additional cost.

- Baltimore City won the prestigious Award for Excellence in Financial Management from the Government Finance Officers Association in 2017 for the OutcomeStat project.

You can learn about more measurable results in the *Results for America* Publication: *Case Study: Baltimore's Advanced Outcome Budgeting System Allows City Leaders to Invest Taxpayer Dollars in Programs and Services That Matter Most.* I've shared the document at SocialSectorHero. com/resources.

Of the many lessons Andrew learned in implementing Outcome Budgeting and OutcomeStat, a few stand out:

- Find and foster your champions. They become viral and can convert — or at least quiet — resisters.

- Be relentless in pursuit of your ideals. A disciplined cycle of planning, budgeting and managing for better outcomes is long, demanding, and sometimes frustrating. But too many organizations take shortcuts or relax their standards, then claim later — when they fall short of the results they hoped for — that the process was flawed.

- Celebrate and communicate small wins, and don't have a quota on telling people "good job."

CHAPTER FOUR ACTION PLAN

Gather some key leaders in your organization, set aside absolutely no more than half a day (four hours maximum) and do the following:

1. Audit the Performance Measures for all of your different grants. While doing this, try to identify any areas of overlap. Also, identify measures that aren't being used. Ask yourself, "What important 'better off' measures might be missing here?" and "How could we better organize these measures under Results or focus areas?"

2. Identify what measures you could remove immediately without any negative consequences. While doing this, prioritize keeping 'better off' measures.

3. Pick one Performance Measure or Community Indicator and create a Turn the Curve Action Plan for it.

4. Ask yourself, "What would need to happen in order for us to start simplifying our performance measurement and reporting systems?" Try to outline some specific steps utilizing the recommendations from our Hero's Journey Spotlights.

CHAPTER 5:

OUTSMART THE DATA TROLL (DISAGGREGATE YOUR DATA FOR TRUE UNDERSTANDING)

"Injustice anywhere is a threat to justice everywhere."
– Martin Luther King, Jr.

When we started Clear Impact 15 years ago, we were not focused on diversity, equity, and inclusion (DEI). Like many technology businesses, we were a predominantly white-male organization. Eventually, we experienced a major shift in our values and priorities thanks to a couple of racial equity heroes — Deena Hayes-Green of the Racial Equity Institute (REI), and Bay Love of the Groundwater Institute.

First, we had all staff attend a two-day racial equity workshop led by Deena and Bay. During this workshop, they presented the case for a "groundwater approach" to racial equity. What we came to better understand is that racism is built into our institutions, structures, and cultures. Furthermore, real change happens when you move away from focusing on personal bigotry and bias, and focus more on changing racist policies, practices, and structures.

Thanks to REI, we all developed a better understanding of the systemic nature of racism. We understood that we needed to work on our policies and practices to be an anti-racist organization. But as many organizations do, we wondered what we should do next. How would we identify what needed to change and then take meaningful action? Being a data-driven organization made our next step clear. We needed to learn more about the state of DEI in our organization using data. Developing and analyzing a new set of DEI Performance Measures revealed areas that needed serious improvement.

To start, we looked at the total number of staff separated by gender and race. This showed us that we needed to increase the percentage of women and people of color in our company as a whole. But as I'll explore with you below, we knew it wasn't enough to look at totals. You must dig deeper into your data to truly understand the circumstances at play in your environment. Digging beyond totals can reveal insights to help you make the most effective decisions possible. To dig deeper, we looked at staff demographics in each department… and a lightbulb exploded! The biggest disparity by far was the composition of our leadership team — all white and all men. This was neither representative of our staff, our clients, nor our communities. We had to prioritize diversification of the leadership team ASAP if we wanted to ensure proper representation and effectiveness.

In the two years before writing this book, we implemented a policy to interview at least one person of color and one woman for every position in every department. I am proud to say that this led to an increase in the percentage of women (now 50 percent) and people of color (now 40 percent) in the company. We also promoted two women to lead the company's marketing, sales, and financial strategies. Racial equity is now one of our official company values and a guiding principle for our work with clients. We have a lot more work to do to fully embody the ideals of anti-racism and racial equity. But I know we can accomplish so much more by continuing to dig deeper into our data.

Avoiding False Guides with Data Disaggregation

Every journey worth taking is fraught with obstacles, dead ends, and enemies bent on destroying the hero's progress. While there are no literal monsters on the Social Sector Hero's journey, there is a troll that can lead you down the wrong path if you aren't careful. This enemy disguises itself as a good-natured guide, but you must resist its lure to avoid becoming distracted and losing your way. Who is this two-faced nemesis? I call it the "superficial data analysis troll." When you fail to consider the multivariate nature of larger data sets, it can negatively impact the whole social sector fellowship. Only looking at total figures in the data allows you to act on faulty — or even dangerous — assumptions.

Lucky for you, there is a shield that can help you ward off this false guide, and the false paths it would lead you down: data disaggregation.

Disaggregating data means taking a single measure — like "Number of program participants" or "Infant survival rate" — and splitting it into multiple measures that reflect particular characteristics or subpopulations. Characteristics are things like race, gender, and socioeconomic status. Subpopulations are things like regions, counties, and neighborhoods. There are endless ways to disaggregate your data. Ultimately, through disaggregation, you are digging deeper into your data to unlock insights that accelerate progress and maximize funding dollars for impact.

Why Bother?

Say you're looking at graduation rates in a region of counties. The superficial data analysis troll may pop out from behind a bush and convince you that your region's graduation rate is 90 percent. You might say, "Wow, that's amazing! It doesn't look like we need to spend a lot of time or money on that right now because we're doing super well. Onward!" So you take a right at the fork in the road instead of a left. But soon enough, you find yourself right back at that fork in the road, facing the same problems and frustrations. Turns out the path to the right is a loop — but the data troll is still there, trying to convince you that the graduation rate is fine, and you just need to try again. At this point though, you know you need to dig a little deeper into the data to figure out the path to success.

At first, you see that each county is doing well. But then you break the data down even further and look at cities. Soon you notice that one city's graduation rate is 25 percent behind the regional average — 65 percent instead of 90 percent. Yikes. You want to get to the bottom of this, so you ask yourself why that city might be struggling. You keep digging deeper, and then it hits you like a slap in the face — one school has just a 40 percent graduation rate, bringing the entire city average down. That's big news, so you don't stop there either — and ask why again. You look at the school with the 40 percent graduation rate and notice that it has a higher percentage of Black teenagers compared to any other school in the region. What does this tell you? Well, asking "why" again is a good start! At least for this school, you need to figure out why Black teenagers aren't graduating at rates similar to their peers so that you can target your strategies accordingly. Similar analysis at other schools in the city — using factors highlighted by disaggregated data — will allow for the creation of additional targeted strategies that will bring the region's graduation rate up even higher. At this point, the troll has disappeared entirely because it knows it won't be able to trick you any more.

Without disaggregating your data like this, you can mask serious disparities in your community. This is the data troll disguising itself with an aggregated data total (e.g. "All people" as opposed to "White people, Black people, Native Americans, Latinx, Asian, Pacific Islander, etc."). The data total may imply good performance or community wellbeing if you look no further — but in reality, there are groups of people that fall behind others nearly 100 percent of the time. This is true whether you're looking at Indicators of community wellbeing or program Performance Measures. It's true whether you're looking at health, education, or financial security. It's true whether you're looking at infrastructure, the environment, or access to transportation. Unless you disaggregate data, you can really lose an important element of your community's story — certain people succeed at much higher rates than others.

If you disaggregate your data, however, you unveil what's really going on. These insights allow you to target services and funding dollars towards those most in need, thus maximizing the impact of your funding. Think about the high school graduation rate scenario. This isn't a fantasy — it's a true story. Many communities face the same racial inequities in educational outcomes. But if you keep asking why, and drilling down into the data to find your answers, you'll eventually get to the root of the problem.

One Small Step for Man, One Giant Leap for Humankind

Remember when we talked about Turn the Curve Thinking? When you engage in Turn the Curve Thinking, the goal is to "turn" the data baseline in the right direction. When you disaggregate measures as often as possible, you can accelerate turning the curve in the right direction. How?

When you unveil disparities, you unlock the ability to create unique strategies for each subpopulation. You can also ensure each strategy is culturally and linguistically appropriate, and that it takes barriers to accessibility into account. You can then begin to optimize the design of your programs to be best suited to the client population.

The theory of "Incrementalism" — first explored by political scientist Charles E. Lindblom — offers evidence in favor of disaggregation.[22] With Incrementalism, you achieve end results through a progression of small steps rather than big, extensively planned jumps. Like RBA, Incrementalism is an intuitive approach; it applies to any journey, regardless of the end goal or application. Incrementalism can help businesses increase profits,

---

22 https://en.wikipedia.org/wiki/Incrementalism

agencies improve community health, people find a new job, and families plan vacations. While it has its disadvantages, Incrementalism, in its most fundamental form, can help you accelerate your journey to social impact with more expediency, simplicity, flexibility, and cooperation.

Consider high school graduation rates again. When we disaggregate this metric by location, school, and/or race, we come to see a multitude of opportunities for incremental progress. We might want to start with just one school at a time and target one subpopulation of students. This is a simpler and more expedient way of Turning the Curve on a regional graduation rate because it involves fewer variables (for now, we only have to worry about designing strategies and programs for one subpopulation). It also prioritizes the variables that have the best chance of maximizing change (if one race has a significantly worse graduation rate, and that rate is significantly improved, the aggregated average will improve faster).

Hero's Journey Spotlight: March of Dimes

Isadora Delvecchio first discovered RBA in 2010 while she was an Elms City Fellow in New Haven, Connecticut. The Fellowship was part of a local leadership development program funded by the Annie E. Casey Foundation. Eventually, Isadora would join the March of Dimes in 2013. After several promotions, she is now their Director of Maternal and Child Health and Collective Impact.

You've probably heard of it, but I love March of Dimes' origin story. There's no way I can improve the story or spice up what they've already shared, so I'll just restate that March of Dimes "has always approached its mission with a spirit of adventure. Born on the eve of World War II as the National Foundation for Infantile Paralysis (NFIP), the Foundation achieved an instantaneous popularity that reflected the contemporary popularity of its founder, Franklin D. Roosevelt."[23] Roosevelt and March of Dimes' social impact journey began with a clear destiny in mind: understanding, curing, and relieving suffering caused by polio through investments in scientific research. Today, March of Dimes fights for the health of all moms and babies — with a focus on maternal health, preterm birth, and closing the health equity gap — by supporting research, programs, education, and advocacy.

As Isadora ascended the organizational mountain of March of Dimes, she realized she needed better data to get clarity in the fight for moms and babies. This would require moving beyond large data sets and taking a multivariate approach. Whether it involved preterm birth, infant mortality, or maternal mortality and morbidity, Isadora knew she would have to hurdle data disaggregation before she could reach effective strategies.

Isadora led an effort to have 30 communities across the United States create baseline data sheets that included clinical and social care data disaggregated by race. This effort told a story of systematic oppression in every single community — Black women have worse experiences when it comes to healthy births. With the urgency created by Black babies dying at much higher rates, March of Dimes performed a root-cause analysis to understand why.

During the analysis, March of Dimes found that the historical impacts of systematic racism across education, legal, and healthcare are significantly driving birth outcomes and causing disproportionate suffering of Black moms and their babies. When overlaying birth outcome maps with old redlining maps in St. Louis, Missouri, March of Dimes found the boundaries to be almost identical. In these communities, there are fewer investments, clinics, hospitals, and transportation options — and these lacking resources are the primary social determinants of health.

---

23 https://www.marchofdimes.org/mission/a-history-of-the-march-of-dimes.aspx

To help communities impacted by institutionalized racism and redlining, March of Dimes created a national equity frame, co-created with 550 community stakeholders, and vetted further by national experts. Through this work, they identified five root causes or areas for improvement:

1. Access to care

2. Quality of care

3. Environmental justice

4. Economic stability

5. Safe and supportive communities.

March of Dimes then asked communities to tailor their solutions to the five root causes and invest dollars accordingly. The goal? Dismantling racism and improving local birth outcomes.

In 2020, March of Dimes implemented RBA Turn the Curve training across partner communities. It's still a bit early to identify measurable improvements, but Isadora reports that the data disaggregation and racial equity efforts have exponentially increased the capacity to run Turn the Curve conversations. Isadora thinks of RBA as "measurement for the people" and that anyone can start down a beautiful data pathway. It's a way to live your values and achieve your priorities through data and data disaggregation.

Isadora was lucky to have an advocate and partner in her fellowship of Social Sector Heroes — March of Dimes President and CEO Stacey Stewart. Stacey championed Isadora's work with RBA, data, racial equity, and Collective Impact. Additionally, she opened the door to name racism as a root cause issue to birth outcomes, as her predecessors did not allow for it. What's the lesson? If you're an Isadora, try to lobby a Stacey. If you're a Stacey, make sure you offer transparent, unapologetic support to the efforts you champion. C-suite buy-in and support for this work are critically important.

"A focus on data gives people a greater sense of clarity in their role," says Isadora. She feels that everyone should disaggregate their data and learn how to use data for decision-making, whether it be via RBA or another framework. These strategies will help you create more powerful plans and allow you to make adjustments as new information emerges.

Where to Dig Deeper — Different Ways to Disaggregate Your Data

There are endless ways to disaggregate your data and categorize groups of people. At Clear Impact, we look at race and gender first, but you're following your own unique journey. You deal with a unique set of circumstances, people, and obstacles. Disparities may not be the same in every community. So, rather than telling you which variables you must disaggregate, let's explore a few possibilities together:

Race

"Approximately 100 million — or 33 percent — of all people in America live in poverty. Nearly 50 percent of people of color live in poverty."[24] – PolicyLink

"In 2019, 70.5 percent of Hispanics had a high school diploma or higher compared to 93.3 percent for non-Hispanic whites. 17.6 percent of Hispanics in comparison had a bachelor's degree or higher compared to 36.9 percent for non-Hispanic whites. 5.6 percent of Hispanics held a graduate or advanced professional degree, compared to 14.3 percent for non-Hispanic whites."[25] – US Department of Health and Human Services, Office of Minority Health

---

24 https://www.policylink.org/resources-tools/moving_from_intention_to_impact

25 https://minorityhealth.hhs.gov/omh/browse.aspx?lvl=3&lvlid=64

Racial inequity is pervasive and ubiquitous. Racism throughout history is built into our societal structures, policies, and institutions. Slavery, Jim Crow, and redlining are just a few of many policies and practices that led to inequitable suffering in Black communities to this day.

If you disaggregate almost any data trend (e.g. infant mortality rate, high school graduation rate, etc.) in any community in America, it shows that some people succeed at higher rates, and some people are much worse off. Generally speaking, White people (and sometimes Asian people) are doing better; Latino, Black, and Native American populations usually fare worse.

Understanding these differences and validating them with data allows local communities to take targeted action towards specific racial subpopulations to close the gaps in wellbeing and success. Wanting all people to succeed — not just advantaged groups — is an important virtue, but also an effective strategy for accelerating social impact.

Gender

"Women and girls in the Americas aged 15+ spend 15.3 percent of their time on unpaid care and domestic work, compared to 9.7 percent spent by men."[26] – UN Women

"In low-middle income countries, one in two women report that they or a woman they know have experienced violence since the COVID-19 Pandemic."[27] – UN Women

---

26 https://data.unwomen.org/country/united-states-of-america

27 https://data.unwomen.org/sites/default/files/documents/Publications/Measuring-shadow-pandemic.pdf

Gender continues to predict a person's well-being and success around the world. Just 102 years ago, women did not have voting rights in the US.[28] For hundreds of years, American women had no legal rights to property ownership or legal authority over their own children. It wasn't until 1900 that every US state gave married women advanced control over their own property.[29] Without the pivotal work of the Women's Suffragette Movement, women may have faced these draconian laws for much longer. It's important to understand here, too, that at first these conditions changed only for White women — it took much longer for Black women and other women of color to make legal gains.

Throughout the twentieth century, women have faced institutionalized discrimination in almost all aspects of life. Women weren't able to apply for credit until the Equal Credit Opportunity Act of 1974.[30] Workplace sexual harassment wasn't legally codified until a series of court proceedings in 1977 thanks to the trailblazing efforts of primarily Black women.[31] Additionally, sexual harassment wasn't officially defined until the 1980s and the commencement of the Equal Employment Opportunity Commission.[32]

Gender discriminatory institutions, policies, structures, and practices like those above have led to inequitable outcomes for women in America and around the world. Today, women and girls suffer when it comes to earning comparable wages as adults. There is no simple cause

---

28 https://www.archives.gov/milestone-documents/19th-amendment

29 https://www.thoughtco.com/property-rights-of-women-3529578

30 https://msmagazine.com/2013/05/28/10-things-that-american-women-could-not-do-before-the-1970s/

31 https://www.legalmomentum.org/newsletters/black-women-trailblazing-all-women

32 https://msmagazine.com/2013/05/28/10-things-that-american-women-could-not-do-before-the-1970s/

and effect here, and the issue is multivariate, but the statistical differences indicate the need for further root-cause analysis.

Socioeconomic Status

"Lower socioeconomic status in childhood is related to poor cognitive development, language, memory, socioemotional processing, and consequently poor income and health in adulthood."[33] – American Psychological Association

"In 2016, the percentage of people enrolled in postsecondary education was 50 percentage points larger for the students in the highest socioeconomic brackets (78 percent) compared to students in the lowest brackets (28 percent)."[34] – *National Center for Education Statistics*

Socioeconomic status is an amalgamation of many variables, including but not limited to income, perceptions of social class, and opportunities. Unfortunately, this means there is no standard definition. A lot of people also confuse race with socioeconomic status when talking about disparities. There is certainly overlap due to historic inequalities. Black people have been systematically denied opportunities to build wealth. But there's an assumption that if someone isn't white, they're automatically from a lower economic status. This isn't always the case.

No matter how you sort out the particulars, most studies show that people of lower socioeconomic status fare worse in educational, financial, and health outcomes. Again, income isn't the only factor, but one piece of the story is intuitive — the less money you have, the less access you have

---

33 https://www.apa.org/pi/ses/resources/publications/education

34 https://nces.ed.gov/programs/coe/indicator/tbe

to the things that make life better. For example, the National Institutes of Health found that as a person's wealth increases so does their health.[35]

Consider that families with higher socioeconomic statuses have more 'gear and guides' to help them navigate the adventures of life. They have access to private schools, tutors, and extra support. Parents with lower socioeconomic statuses have a much tougher time supporting their children's educational journey. They may have multiple jobs, and they may not have the time or money to enroll their kids in after-school programs. They may not even know about programs since they don't have access to a computer and nobody bothered to mail the pamphlets!

Ability/Disability

"61 million Americans — 26 percent of adults — in the United States have some type of disability. Disabilities are more common for certain groups — older adults, women, minorities, and those living in the Southern States."[36] – Centers for Disease Control

"In July 2019, almost half of all persons with a disability who were not working reported some type of barrier to employment (the disability itself, lack of education or training, lack of transportation, and the need for special features at the job)."[37] – US Bureau of Labor Statistics

Both of my parents have worked to help people with disabilities for their entire careers, which has made me acutely aware of many of the issues people with disabilities routinely face. What I've learned throughout my social impact journey is that people with disabilities are largely shut out of the

---

35 https://www.ncbi.nlm.nih.gov/pmc/articles/PMC7314918/

36 https://www.cdc.gov/ncbddd/disabilityandhealth/infographic-disability-impacts-all.html

37 https://www.bls.gov/news.release/dissup.nr0.htm

workforce system. For example, researchers at Cornell University determined that in 2018, only 37.8 percent of all non-institutionalized people with a disability aged 21-64 were employed in the United States.[38] In the same year, 60.6 percent of all people in the United States were employed — a 62.3 percent disparity.

Employers hold the key to unlocking this statistic, so they have a special responsibility to educate themselves. Most employers who decide to hire someone with a disability do so for a couple of reasons: 1) they have previous experience hiring someone with a disability, and/or 2) they have personal relationships with people with disabilities (co-workers, friends, family, etc.). For employers without personal experience and/or relationships, the main sources of education tend to be popular culture and media (books, movies, etc.). There is also a lack of awareness of different types of disabilities and differences in severity within each disability sub-category.[39]

Due to the disparities, targeted strategies should aim to increase inclusion for people with disabilities. Ideally, we want all people to be independent, self-sufficient, and maintain stable and fulfilling employment — regardless of disability type or status. You can't expect someone to climb a mountainside by themselves with no gear, and you can't leave them behind. Assisting the other people on our journey isn't just the right thing to do — what if they have knowledge that you don't have, that you need to overcome future obstacles on the road to social impact?

Social Sector Heroes in the workforce development community are leading the charge for change by identifying job industries where people with different disabilities tend to thrive and increasing access to those people. Employment is so important because it directly relates to a person's

---

38 https://www.disabilitystatistics.org/reports/acs.cfm?statistic=2

39 https://www.ncbi.nlm.nih.gov/pmc/articles/PMC8156639/

access to services, community inclusion, social fulfillment, and creating meaning in life.

The Intersectional Nature of Disparities

Whether you're a disaggregation warrior or just learning the tools of the trade, there's always room for improvement. Say you're progressing along your journey to social impact. Even when you think you've analyzed every possible obstacle and dodged every false guide, you can still wander down ineffective pathways. Why? Well, sometimes there is an even deeper level of disaggregation you may be missing. This is the intersectional nature of disparity. Oftentimes, we can't just look at gender disparities; we also need to examine racial-gender disparities. We can't just look at ability/ disability status; we need to look at race and ability/disability status. Many people experience several types of disparity, and the effect is often that the whole is greater than the sum of the parts.

The data shows us that if we couple race with another categorization, people of color usually fare worse than their peers within the original disaggregated group. Remember when we were talking about the employment rate for people with disabilities? It was 38.7 percent. When you disaggregate that total by race, you see that only 16 percent of Black people with disabilities are employed[40] — that's more than a 50 percent reduction from the total! This is only the tip of the iceberg.

What about race and gender? According to research out of the UK, women as a whole are disproportionately likely to be remanded compared to men, and Black and other minority women even more so: "Black women [are] much more likely than white women to be given custodial sentences

---

40 https://clearimpact.com/resources/turnthecurve-examples/smart-incentives/

for the same offenses." [41] OK — we are two for two. What about race and socioeconomic status? While all households for every race experienced an increase in household income from 2018 to 2019, the rate of increase differed among races. Asians fared the best with a 10.6 percent increase, but the rate for Hispanic households was behind at 7.1 percent. White households had the smallest increase at 5.7 percent, but their average household income was still 65 percent higher than Black households. [42]

When you integrate intersectionality into your data analysis, you will generally disaggregate by two levels. For example, when you look at employment rate (or any other Indicator of wellbeing or program performance measure) you can disaggregate it by two different variables — first by ability/disability status, and then by race (or whichever variables you want to understand). The more specific you can get with your data and the better you get at intersectionality, the more targeted, and thus more effective your strategies become, and the higher the return on social investment your fellowship can attain.

Hero's Journey Spotlight: Whatcom County

Whatcom County is in the northwestern corner of Washington State and shares a border with Canada, as well as two indigenous tribes: the Lummi Nation and the Nooksack Tribe. They are deeply connected to the mountains (North Cascades) and waterways (the Salish Sea and many rivers) that have been protected by native tribes since time immemorial. The county's population is roughly 230,000 and predominantly White (86.2

---

41 https://weareagenda.org/bame-women-face-double-disadvantage-in-criminal-justice-system/

42 https://www.epi.org/blog/racial-disparities-in-income-and-poverty-remain-largely-unchanged-amid-strong-income-growth-in-2019/

percent). As is the case throughout the country, this isn't by accident but by historical design.

Community Health Improvement is a best practice for Health Departments and a requirement to be nationally accredited by the Public Health Accreditation Board. Knowing this, Whatcom County got to work developing an anti-racist, community-driven process to create a Community Health Assessment that resulted in a Community Health Improvement Plan (CHIP). Led by Amy Rydel, Health Planning Specialist at the Whatcom County Health Department, the Healthy Whatcom Team convened for the first time in 2017. This team is a cross-sector group of stakeholders guiding the community health improvement process to advance racial justice and develop the County's CHIP.

This work would not have been possible without early investments from the Chuckanut Health Foundation (CHF), Mount Baker Foundation (MBF), PeaceHealth, and Whatcom Community Foundation. CHF established a fund for community health improvement that other funders could pay into called the Healthy Whatcom Fund. This created a flexible funding source and removed barriers — through compensation for participation and expertise — for individuals with personal experiences of racism, marginalization, or difficulty trying to access the systems the County is trying to change. MBF provided the funds to use technology for the Turn the Curve conversations using disaggregated data from the beginning of the journey.

In 2018, Whatcom completed a Community Health Assessment to better understand experiences with health and wellbeing in the county. After disaggregating their data by race, they unveiled a pattern. The pattern told a story of people of color being disproportionately impacted across all systems (education, health care, child welfare, criminal, legal, etc.). Whatcom didn't have a people problem — they had a systems problem.

In 2019, Whatcom County gathered over 100 community members together to share the quantitative data alongside community member stories and personal experiences. They then went through a facilitated process to identify the top three priorities for collaborative community action, with racial equity threaded through each priority:

1. Child and youth mental health
2. Early learning and child care
3. Housing for children and families.

Before jumping into action, the Healthy Whatcom team examined each priority and the work already happening. In doing so, they realized that there was a tremendous amount of work underway — but it wasn't having the intended impact. This brought them to RBA and collaboration with Marcos Marquez at Clear Impact. They also engaged with the Racial Equity Institute (mentioned earlier in this chapter), a nationally-renowned organization focused on anti-racism and undoing structural racism. The goal? To incorporate community learning about systemic racism and undoing systems of oppression *before* they developed their Action Plans.

An RBA workshop brought practical, actionable, and methodical approaches to planning, implementation, and evaluation. The addition of REI's groundwater workshop helped the team determine which evidence-based interventions would truly address racist structures, policies, and institutions. Combining RBA and REI blended the strength of science with the collective wisdom of lived experiences — all grounded in trust. The team was more ready than ever to bring creative, brave, and frankly, under-researched solutions to address racial inequity.

Then COVID struck, and the work was paused for almost a year, but in May 2021, Healthy Whatcom resumed its efforts with a series of Zoom strategic planning workshops with over 140 community partners. Together, they used RBA to develop community-driven and community-centered Action Plans for child and youth mental health, housing, and early learning and child care. These Action Plans became Whatcom County's CHIP.

Understanding the importance of 'less is more', Healthy Whatcom began by looking at kindergarten readiness disaggregated by race and ethnicity during the workshops. What they found was that about half of all children were entering kindergarten ready to learn. When they dug deeper and disaggregated by race, they found that children of color were half as likely to enter kindergarten ready to learn as their white peers.

During the Zoom workshops, community members came together to dig into the early-learning data, and asked themselves — what's the story behind the disparity? In this case, inclusion was the key to unlocking the answer. For Healthy Whatcom, how they do their work is just as important as the work itself. To eliminate inequities and advance racial justice in each phase of community health improvement, Healthy Whatcom strives to shift power to communities of color, make systems-level change, and center the voices and experiences of community members who are Black, Indigenous, and other People of Color. As a result, they intentionally ensured that participants in these workshops brought a mix of personal experiences of racism, marginalization, and/or access to systems they were trying to change. They also included people with resources and power *within* the systems to make a change.

Healthy Whatcom completed its CHIP in March 2022 and began launching its action teams. The processes they developed through RBA workshops — especially including disaggregation of data — moved forward with them into implementation. To ensure their work continues to demonstrate their values during implementation, they are collaborating with funders to develop processes, like participatory budgeting exercises, that shift power into the hands of those with lived experience to decide where and how resources are allocated. This will help create flexible funding streams and shift the "fighting for crumbs" mindset to one of collaborative fundraising.

Whatcom County's work is in its early phases, just as it is over at March of Dimes. At the time of writing, it is a bit early to see turned curves.

But Whatcom is creating better, targeted CHIP strategies with a multi-layered disaggregation of data. In short, disaggregate *before* strategizing. Their work also shows us that RBA is a flexible framework that can incorporate and elevate anti-racism and equity work to move communities forward.

Don't Forget — Minimize the Side-Quests

I already gave the 'less is more' mindset its own chapter, but it's really applicable to every tip in this book. Incrementalism — or the addition of small steps over time — is also useful in data disaggregation efforts. Take a cue from Whatcom County's story and organize your journey map into bite-size chunks of data analysis, capacity-building, collaboration, and implementation. Don't do everything all at once — you'll just get confused and burned out.

To realize your social sector destiny and achieve results, it's always best to start small. Start by collecting and disaggregating data for one Indicator or Performance Measure at a time. Then, expand this effort once you have built up your disaggregation and equity "muscles". This will help you unlock important insights, target resources toward those most affected, ensure equity in your service delivery, and create a greater impact for everyone combined.

CHAPTER 5 ACTION PLAN

Here's how you and your funded partners can start thwarting data trolls, disaggregating data to gain a deeper understanding of your ultimate path to progress:

1. Do a scan of the nine Indicators in PolicyLink's National Equity Atlas (accessible at SocialSectorHero.com/Resources) and figure out if you'd like to help to Turn the Curve on any of the Indicators. If none of these Indicators interest you, pick any Indicator or Performance Measure that you're passionate about.

2. Read *Racial Equity: Getting to Results* (accessible at SocialSectorHero.com/Resources), by Erica Bernabei and published by the Government Alliance for Racial Equity. This publication will help you connect a racial equity lens to the Results-Based Accountability (RBA) and Turn the Curve methodology.

3. Create a Turn the Curve plan for your chosen Indicator or Performance Measure. In your data analysis and plan, disaggregate the data by one variable. See what kind of story the first four steps of the plan tell. If you're not happy with the story, finish the Turn the Curve Plan and create a targeted strategy to make a difference.

4. Optional: Read *DEI Made Measurable* (accessible at SocialSectorHero.com/resources) for ideas on measuring DEI and perceptions of DEI within your own organization. If you're interested in enhancing your understanding of racial equity and racism, I highly recommend Racial Equity Institute's workshops.

CHAPTER 6:
MULTIPLE PATHS TO THE SUMMIT
(BE CONSISTENT AND FLEXIBLE)

"True flexibility can be achieved only when all muscles are uniformly developed." —Joseph Pilates

My four kids have wildly different personalities. One is extremely shy, one is outgoing, one goes along to get along, and one prefers to just be left alone. What they have in common, however, are shared genetics and the amount of love we have for them. My wife and I try to maintain consistency in our parenting style and the same general expectations when it comes to how the kids treat us, themselves, and other people.

Consistency is one thing, but fairness is another. What does it mean to be fair? For me, it means that the way we define and measure success for each kid is flexible — tailored to their personality, values, and aspirations. We want them each to have an equal opportunity to succeed and grow as individuals. We also want them to have fun and derive fulfillment from whatever they're doing. We also need to be flexible with the support we give, as each kid thrives on different words of encouragement, resources, and routines.

Flexibility in these areas is critical in accommodating each kid's differences in interests, goals, communications styles, perspectives, skills, preferred behaviors, and aspirations. When you serve as someone's primary support system, you're going to have to rely on your own experience and values to guide them. But I have to let my kids be the heroes of their own stories. This involves allowing them to take part in designing the means to achieving my expectations and theirs.

For example, my wife and I are consistent in our expectations about behavior, participation in sports, and academic achievement. If the kids had Performance Measures, they might look something like this:

- Number of times they demonstrated kindness to a sibling

- Percentage of sports practices attended during the week

- Homework completion rate

Given their unique personalities, they may each have a few additional Performance Measures that are specific to them. These might look like:

- Shy:
  » Number of times they embraced a new social situation
  » Number of times they raised their hand in class

- Outgoing:
  » Number of times they actively listened to others
  » Number of times they interrupted their classroom by talking

- Goes along to get along:
  » Number of times they took initiative to do something by themselves
  » Number of times they took a leadership role on a sports team or in a classroom

- Prefers to be left alone:
  - » Number of times they left their room and engaged with a family member
  - » Number of friends they invited over to play

I have to emphasize — we don't actually use these Performance Measures at home. And it's OK to be outgoing, quiet, easygoing, independent, or any combination of these. We aren't trying to change their personalities. Rather, we are encouraging them to build resiliency and become well-rounded individuals. These are skills that will help any hero reach their personal destiny. My main point is that there are endless ways of becoming resilient. To successfully navigate the world around them and achieve whatever "success" means to them, each kid might need a different journey map. But they also need consistent guidance from their parents.

Similarly, each of your different funded partners need consistency and flexibility to achieve success and meet your expectations. The main way to do this is to establish a handful of similar measures for each comparable set of programs (e.g. all mentoring programs, all workforce training programs, or all after-school programs). You can then aggregate these measures to tell a story of impact for the entire fellowship. Additionally, you should always give your partners the flexibility to report an additional handful of measures that reflect their unique goals and communities.

Consistency: The Skeleton Key to Progress

Consistency = everyone doing everything the same way (or everyone doing a core set of things the same way), in the interest of accelerating progress on the Common Purpose.

You are a trusted guide for your funded partners and community — a wise sage that has uncovered the keys to progress. These keys are your accumulated knowledge, power, resources, vision, and unique position to facilitate alignment. Every partner needs the same key to break down obstacles and reach the next stage of their impact adventure. Make sure you are consistent when it comes to sharing your keys.

In more practical terms, this means defining consistent Performance Measures across like programs. For example, if you're looking at an after-school program or have a series of after-school programs, each should have two or three consistent measures. Besides telling your aggregate story of impact, identical Performance Measures allow you to quickly gain a sense of whether or not your investments in each individual partner were worth it.

What happens when you're consistent? Imagine you were a college professor. You have consistent objectives for your entire class and want everyone to achieve a core set of learning outcomes. But instead of teaching the same 45-minute lesson plan to all 25 of your students at once, you have to teach a different lesson plan to each individual student. You'd have to hold a 45-minute class with each student and each lesson would present the information in a different way. Imagine the horror!

There's a reason higher education doesn't operate this way. You wouldn't even have enough time to sleep or eat if you had to teach this way. But it's not just a matter of time — it's a matter of measurement. If you teach every student in one aggregate class, using the same lesson plan, assignments, and syllabus, you're able to measure success in the same exact way and tell a larger story of your impact as a professor.

It works the same way for your social impact fellowship. If you all have the same Common Purpose, Indicators, Performance Measures, and frameworks, you're going to save yourself so much time. Why? You'll only have to teach everyone one simple system — instead of multiple complex systems. This is also true when looking inward to your own organization and staff. If you're consistent across the board, staff turnover will leave you less vulnerable to invasive frameworks, ill-suited technologies, and inefficient systems.

Flexibility: Where Paths Diverge

Flexibility = People can be creative in how they design strategies, measure success, tell their story, and do the on-the-ground work in support of the Common Purpose.

You probably realize by now that I love numbers. Unfortunately, in terms of statistics on flexibility, not much data exists specific to the context of the funder-grantee relationship. However, there is evidence that suggests people prefer some level of flexibility when it comes to their professional lives. In 2018, Workest, a business intelligence technology company, interviewed hundreds of businesses and found that 73 percent of employees felt that flexible work arrangements increased their satisfaction at work, while an even higher number, 78 percent, felt that flexibility made them more productive.[43] I'm comfortable making the leap that there's probably a similarity between private-sector employees and employees in the public and social sectors.

Imagine you funded three after-school programs that operate in generally the same way but have different focus areas. One might introduce kids to sports. One might focus on reading. One might promote the arts. So, while you'll want to track things like attendance rate, program quality, and impact on academic performance, you might need specific measures per focus area. One of the reasons is that promoting sports, art, and reading all contain inherent value outside of any desire to improve academic measures of achievement (even though they're often contributory).

I once worked with an organization that funded between 30 and 40 different mentoring programs at any given time. In trying to figure out a performance management reporting system across partners, we realized that mentoring was delivered differently. Sometimes, it was delivered in

---

43 https://www.zenefits.com/workest/7-big-statistics-about-the-state-of-flexible-work-arrangements/

a group setting and sometimes it was one-on-one. To account for these differences, we came up with three consistent measures across all the programs and 20 optional measures that partners could select based on their mode of operation. With this, each partner could maintain focus on the fellowship's goals and values while also telling their unique story of community impact.

As long as you've got some core standards like goals and values, you can be extremely flexible on how partners align with and achieve these standards. Allow people to be creative in the "means" to your "ends." Flexibility increases the chances you'll discover new and different strategies to create impact. At the end of the day, flexibility creates uniqueness and invites innovation that accelerates progress.

Hero's Journey Spotlight: United Way of Waco-McLennan County

If you've ever heard of Chip and Joanna Gaines and their show "Fixer Upper", you're probably familiar with Waco, Texas. Their home base is Crawford, Texas — located just on the outskirts of Waco. Nearby, in the heart of Waco resides the United Way of Waco-McLennan County (UWWMC).

UWWMC is a relatively small United Way — there are six staff and 33 funded programs across 22 partners. But we all know great things come in small packages. UWWMC and its partners reached an aggregated 4,777 children, adults, and families in 2021 through the programs they support,[44] despite the impacts of COVID-19. Even more impressive was the fact that 82 percent of clients were determined to be better off as a result of UWWMC-supported programming.

----

44 https://www.unitedwaywaco.org/

A few years ago, UWWMC realized their community's financial stability was suffering. Notably, Waco's poverty rate was 26.8 percent, representing more than twice the national average. A look at the data, disaggregated by race and ethnicity, also told them 24 percent of African-Americans and 21 percent of Latinx people lived in poverty compared to 12 percent of white people. To address these realities, UWWMC began to pursue innovative approaches to measurable progress.

UWWMC staff were first introduced to Results-Based Accountability and Clear Impact's services in 2018 as a means to take an aligned and collaborative approach to community data collection. Along with community partners, UWWMC agreed that they would adopt the framework as it aligned perfectly with their goals and values. They had just experienced a change in organizational leadership, and with the new project leadership of Tiffani Johnson, Senior Director for Impact and Engagement, there was a refreshed interest in aligning grantees for impact.

To get the gears turning, UWWMC gathered their grantees and asked them about the goals they wanted for the community — these turned into the community priorities of:

- Education: Children have the skills and knowledge to succeed in school and life

- Financial Stability: Individuals and families have the ability to improve their financial stability and economic status

- Health: Individuals and families can improve their health and live healthy lives

- Safety Net Services: Individuals and families can meet their essential needs to move out of crisis situations.

UWWMC also created a task force of community leaders and consulted the United Way Worldwide Global Results Framework — mentioned in the Hero's Journey Spotlight in Chapter Four — to ensure alignment with the United Way network as a whole. They envisioned future collaborative alignment with other local foundations to advance towards a grand, community-wide vision of data collection. They shared my dream of a massive, cross-sector, cohesive force for social impact.

At the end of the day, UWWMC successfully aligned its grantees with a Common Purpose: strengthening their community by mobilizing resources towards the shared focus areas of education, health, financial stability, and safety net services. How would they all align with the vision and achieve the mission? Everyone had to commit to collaborating, inspiring wider participation and giving, engaging the community, mobilizing resources towards impact, promoting public awareness, and demonstrating transparency and accountability.

When I spoke with UWWMC's Tiffani Johnson, her two big tips for success aligned with the values of consistency and flexibility in performance management and reporting. First, when getting started, she suggested that funders give one to two years of lead time for grantees to get used to performance expectations and reporting. This should happen before funders start evaluating the metrics. Wiggle room allows for a high level of flexibility for organizations to gather their data, work out the kinks in their data collection systems, and get used to the idea and practice of regular performance reporting.

Second, funders should provide partners with a common data reporting system. This helps standardize reporting activities, streamline data collection for the funder, and ultimately allows funders to aggregate performance data to communicate shared impact. For UWWMC, their common reporting tool reinforced the use of a common language and framework to enhance a spirit of fellowship and inclusion in a grander purpose.

To demonstrate the value of UWWMC's new social impact framework (beyond that of a reporting exercise), they created consistent learning opportunities for partners to improve their understanding and implementation of Results-Based Accountability and outcomes measurement via annual training. They also maintained cohesion by developing common goals, focus areas, and performance metrics. Throughout the journey, patience and flexibility helped engage UWWMC's partners in new initiatives. They understood the value and power of giving grantees a space to report on a few metrics that spoke to their uniqueness.

While the COVID-19 pandemic skewed the data due to temporary program closures, strong outcomes were produced across UWWMC's grantee network in 2021. These results were influenced by consistent Performance Measures and reporting systems across similar programs, outlined below.

"Pillar" Outcomes (Highest Level of Outcome Data Aggregation Across Like Programs):

- 79 percent of families and children served by programs in the Education pillar improved their knowledge and skills in order to be successful in school and life

- 91 percent of clients served by programs in the Financial Stability pillar improved their financial stability and economic status

- 87 percent of clients served by programs in the Health pillar improved their health and ability to live healthy lives

- 71 percent of individuals and families served by programs in the Safety Net Services pillar were able to meet their essential needs in order to move out of crisis.

2021 Goal and Objective Area Outcomes:

- 85 percent of children served made progress toward achieving social-emotional developmental milestones

- 93 percent of clients served increased their knowledge and skills in order to obtain jobs with the potential for advancement

- 85 percent of individuals served increased their knowledge and skills to improve their overall health and wellness

- 71 percent of individuals served received the services and resources needed to meet their basic needs in crisis situations.

UWWMC aggregates these metrics in their common performance reporting system — the Clear Impact Scorecard. The Scorecard provides an automated system that helps UWWMC communicate impact in the four focus areas. It allows partners to instantly update data remotely, which is then instantly aggregated into larger Impact Framework Scorecards. The Scorecard allows UWWMC to more easily answer the following questions:

- How much work are partners doing?

- How are residents better off as a result of that work?

- Are there different gains in education, financial stability, health, or safety net services?

- What do the individual contributions of partners mean at an aggregate level?

Following UWWMC's example, funders should take the time to work one-on-one with each grantee to define measures that are actionable and accurately tell their program's story — not just a laundry list of throw-away measures. And whether it's the Clear Impact Scorecard, another software, or an in-house system, everyone should use the same reporting process.

You can learn more about UWWMC's initiatives and progress in their official case study at SocialSectorHero.com/Resources.

Always Keep a Lookout: Opportunities for Implementation

Consistency and flexibility don't just apply to performance management. These principles show up everywhere from the big things (investment decisions, measuring shared outcomes, strategizing) to the small things (daily operations, sending emails, designing grant applications, etc.). This is not a complete list, but I've put together some areas where it's important to integrate a little bit of consistency and a little bit of flexibility.

Language

Consistency in language is like utilizing the same exact map and legend for everyone on a social impact journey. When you utilize consistent terminology or a 'common language', you allow people to communicate with each other simply. Everyone can easily identify, point out, and discuss obstacles, paths to progress and destinations. When apples = apples for everyone, you'll waste less time explaining how systems and methodologies work, and you'll have less confusion and miscommunication. Whether you use the language of Results-Based Accountability or any other framework, make sure it's consistent in all that you do — whether you're working internally or externally.

How can you be consistent and flexible with language at the same time? As long as the language you use is consistent and everyone understands it, you can be flexible in the actual terms you use. Consider this question — what do you call a condition of wellbeing for children, adults, and families? Does everyone in your organization use the same term? What about your grantees? I use Results-Based Accountability, so my term for that idea is "Result." You could call it "Outcomes" or anything you want, as long as everyone in the organization understands what each term means.

Frameworks

Using a consistent framework (or frameworks) for creating social change, making budgeting decisions, and performance improvement allows for better capacity-building, organizational alignment, and smaller learning curves. Similar to language, it doesn't matter what framework you use, as long as it's the same for everyone. Consistent frameworks allow you to make aligned decisions and aggregate your story of impact.

One way flexibility may arise is when you use different frameworks for different purposes. If you want to visually represent your work, a logic model or a theory of change might make sense, but you wouldn't want to blend them together with another framework. Use one framework per purpose. Another way to incorporate flexibility is to allow some wiggle room in how you implement a framework chronologically. Frameworks are not religions and you're not doomed to a fiery inferno if you choose to do things in a particular order or (gasp) skip a step that isn't useful to you. Just get started where you're at, given the time, resources, and information at your disposal. You can always come back to skipped steps later. Remember, you don't have to have all the data to take action.

Grantmaking

The simplest way to implement consistency in grantmaking is to make grant applications identical and provide a rubric to guide the grantee. This will allow evaluators to grade applications with the same objective measures. It will also allow you to more easily compare the quality of one application to another, leading to better investment decisions.

Similar to Performance Measures, there might be unique elements to your applicants that can help you better evaluate opportunities to maximize impact. So, in your applications, have an open-ended section like, "Tell us anything else that you think is important for us to know when evaluating your application." Don't be prescriptive or lead the applicant towards a certain answer. And give them ample space to make their case.

Performance Reporting

Once you know what your Performance Measures are, how they're reported is equally important. Consistency in your performance reporting system creates a common way of looking at the data. You don't want one group submitting a pie chart, the other group submitting a line chart, and another group submitting a bar chart. You want to be able to look at the data in the same way *and* in the same place in order to improve your decision-making.

Numbers and measures are one thing, and there aren't many opportunities for flexibility (other than allotting each partner a few optional or unique measures). Where flexibility definitely shows up, however, is in the narrative that goes with the measures. This is the "Story Behind the Curve" or the contextual information that helps you to understand why the data looks the way it does. You should never ask for data without giving people a place to report on the story and context.

Tools and Technologies

Consistency in tools and technologies means every one of your grantees is using the same Data Management System to report data to you. I would even go so far as to recommend you mandate that partners use the system to be considered for a grant. One centralized system allows for better analysis between programs. It also increases the ease of navigation and organization of your data.

Think about if you were going on some sort of sailing expedition across a vast sea. You'd want everyone in your fellowship to either be in the same boat or multiples of the same boat. It's no good if some boats go faster than others, some are vulnerable to lightning strikes, or some are armed and others are not. But if everyone is using the same boat — or technology — you can all go in the same direction, at the same speed, at the same relative distance from one another, with the same equipment. It creates alignment and cohesion. Similarly, a common data management software system allows you to organize all of your information in one easily accessible place and compare everyone's progress.

Here, flexibility comes in the form of the qualitative information grantees include when they report data to the common system. This is why it's so important to choose a system that provides a space for custom notes and narratives with every metric (in the individual data points themselves and for the data trendline as a whole).

If you come across a data collection system that automatically feeds data into your preferred Performance Management System, this is another opportunity to implement consistency in the form of mandates. Finally, if you're going to require the use of technology, make sure you offer capacity-building, training, and support on the effective use of those systems. Not everyone you're going to work with is technically savvy or familiar with the available systems. Providing advanced support will get you more buy-in, more consistent usage of the systems (e.g. logging in daily or weekly as opposed to monthly), and optimized usage of the systems (e.g. accessibility of advanced features to help accelerate your impact).

Hero's Journey Spotlight:
Brighter Futures and Child Youth and Family Services

Beth Stockton is an evaluator, community builder, and facilitator with The Jeder Institute and Collaboration for Impact. She has decades of experience advocating for child wellbeing in cities around the world like Sydney, London, and San Mateo. In 2016, Beth realized many child and youth-focused funders have trouble measuring outcomes across their funding streams and programs. So, she reflected on her experiences in an article for the Clear Impact blog. In that piece, she recounted helping a regional family services agency in Australia to create consistency in their performance measurement.

In the early 2010s in the state of New South Wales (NSW), NSW Family Services Incorporated (Fams) worked with 16 Brighter Futures Lead Agencies across NSW and 10 Child Youth and Family Services (CYFS) in the Nepean Blue Mountains District of the state. The goal? According to Beth, the funders wanted to see if it was possible to meaningfully measure shared outcomes across funding streams.

Prior to Fams' involvement with Brighter Futures (an early inter-vention program for children who are at high risk of entering or escalating within the child protection system), the agencies were already collecting significant amounts of required data. However, they reported that the data was not telling them whether they were actually improving outcomes for their clients. The funders also reported that the data they were getting was inaccurate and, therefore, not useful for programming decisions and reporting to the State Treasury.

Fams led an outcomes-focused overhaul to help CYFS and Brighter Futures get on the same page. Around this time, Beth had served as a Policy Consultant for Fams and was currently serving as an Outcomes Measurement and Learning Development Specialist delivering RBA train-ing and facilitation. Beth and her fellow Social Sector Heroes at Fams were able to uncover two primary reasons the data collection wasn't working. These were issues common to the field in general.

Throughout her work, Beth found that measurement is most effec-tive and meaningful when funders are consistent and flexible with grantees when measuring shared outcomes. To help funders get better at measure-ment, Beth outlines two main data inconsistency pitfalls, a process for developing effective Performance Measures, and methods for collecting and evaluating shared measures. I will summarize her findings below (you can read the full article at SocialSectorHero.com/Resources).

Data Pitfalls

According to Beth, funders should avoid the following big mistakes:

Measures That are Too Specific

Even for agencies and programs focused on children and families, the nature of the work the organizations do is incredibly diverse. Usually, success comes from meeting a family at their point of need. When funders are too prescriptive about all measures that a grantee should collect, the measures do not always capture the primary area of need for the family.

Unclear Language

When an organization is collecting data for the purpose of internal quality improvement, it is critical that they are clear on what data they are collecting and why. This involves clear language and communication across the organization, particularly with those involved in collecting the data. In order for data to be meaningful, it's important each organization interprets the measure the same way and collects the *exact* same thing.

Tips for Avoiding Data Pitfalls

Funders should embed processes that support organizations for clarifying purposes, identifying outcomes, and designing Performance Measures into the work. A useful set of steps to guide this process includes:

- Train organizations and funders in Results-Based Accountability and build buy-in

- Collaborate and agree to a set of Performance Measures that will best represent the outcomes that you are trying to achieve

- Discuss the language of each measure to ensure that every organization understands what data they are collecting and why

- Recognize the limitations caused by averaging data across multiple organizations using different data collection tools/systems

- Focus on each organization's individual data for quality improvement planning

- Use the Results-Based Accountability framework for ongoing quality improvement

- Support each organization to capture data regularly and enter the data into a web-based performance management program

- Continue to have conversations about data collection to ensure that it remains useful.

Beth believes that funders can also meaningfully measure shared outcomes by limiting the number of mandatory shared measures and giving grantees the autonomy to develop additional measures meaningful to their own quality improvement. She noticed that when partner organizations are allowed a degree of autonomy to measure, analyze and report back on outcomes specific to their programs, they are more invested in using data for genuine learning and quality improvement, as opposed to data for reporting purposes only.

What were the results of utilizing consistent language and making space for autonomy in measures? Beth shares that organizational leaders with Brighter Futures and CYFS are now driven to use outcomes measurement as a tool to:

1. Clearly redefine why their organization exists and why they do what they do

2. Support the organization to 'show up differently' and work innovatively, with sights set on outcomes as opposed to counting activities

3. Guide their organization to think outwardly, striving to better understand how their work contributes to the broader aspirational goals of the community they serve.

To summarize this chapter and Beth's advice, consistency, particularly in Performance Measures and Performance Reporting systems, can help you compare the effectiveness of different investments. This is difficult, but one way to accomplish consistency is to create a few standardized measures for similar programs.

Every organization, community, and program is unique, so it's important that partners have the flexibility to design appropriate strategies that reflect their unique circumstances, skills, and resources. They should have the opportunity to report on optional unique measures and tell their detailed data story. Consistency and flexibility allow you to realize the maximum potential of your investments, tell your fellowship's story of aggregate impact, and highlight the differences, roles, and accomplishments that make you all indispensable to your stakeholders.

CHAPTER SIX ACTION PLAN

1. Take a subset of your grantees that have similar programs and have a conversation about how to measure performance. See if you can all come to a consensus on three meaningful measures they could all report on.

2. Evaluate available software systems to figure out a common platform for performance reporting and/or data collection.

3. Figure out how you can make life easier for yourself, your fellow funders, and your grantees through collaborative systems and frameworks. To start, reach out to some funders to see how they are measuring grantee performance. Identify any potential areas of overlap where you could both utilize the same measures, thus streamlining the grantees' performance reporting across funders and enhancing a spirit of collaboration and shared vision in your community.

CHAPTER 7:
JOURNALING THE JOURNEY (NEVER REPORT ON DATA WITHOUT THE STORY)

"Get it down. Take chances. It may be bad, but it's the only way you can do anything really good." – William Faulkner

Maintaining a healthy weight has been a challenge for most of my adult life. For a long time, my weight fluctuated 30 to 40 pounds, up or down. The rollercoaster was at its most gut-wrenching when I willfully avoided the scale. It was the elephant in the bathroom. Later, I realized this was making things much worse, so I committed myself to paying attention to the data and accepting it for what it was. This simple act unlocked my ability to engage in an authentic analysis. The scale wasn't trying to personally offend me and neither was the number on it. It was just data.

Once I accepted the situation, I could think objectively (even dispassionately) and get down to business. I started asking myself questions and giving honest answers in return, no matter how painful. What was really causing the instability in my weight? Were my meals too big? Was I snacking too much? Drinking too much? Working out inconsistently? Were my workouts intense enough? Was I capable of doing more? Was I making excuses? How much time could I realistically dedicate to my experiment and analysis?

Rome wasn't built in a day and neither was my weight loss journey. Over the course of a year, here's what I found out. When I step on the scale, it allows me to intentionally think about 1) is anything better than it was yesterday, and 2) what can I do better today? If nothing got better after a week of weigh-ins, obviously, I wasn't doing something right. I needed to course-correct. The first step in any journey is to be mindful of where you're at and think about the "story behind the data." So what was the story behind the number on the scale?

For the most part, I've been fairly consistent with exercise. At one time, I was walking a couple of miles every single day. I started going to the gym and lifting weights. I still do those things because they have amazing benefits. But it wasn't enough. I clearly didn't have the whole story because I still hadn't met my goals. It was then that I realized I wasn't very conscious about what I was eating. I was exercising a lot, but it wasn't making a difference. So I began examining the data points of my diet — identifying what, how much, how quickly or slowly, and how often I ate. This helped me understand the story behind the data: *why* I was eating that way, and as a result, which experiments might be fruitful.

One of the experiments I tried was intermittent fasting — basically shortening the window of time in which you consume food throughout the day. Once I started doing this, the extra weight slowly started to come off and stay off. With intermittent fasting, I've been able to consistently maintain a healthier weight for three years. Now, this is not a nutrition book and I'm not making any dietary recommendations here. What I *am* recommending is analyzing the story behind your data (whether it be an Indicator or Performance Measure) before taking action. Without slowing down to examine my nutrition story, I may have continued to trudge through increasingly intense workouts without switching up my eating habits. But by objectively acknowledging and analyzing my data instead,

I've saved countless hours and huge amounts of energy, and have reached my goals faster.

Imagine if your grantees were, like me, too scared to get on the scale and measure their performance. Or if they sent you a bunch of numbers without any context. It would be like sending you their weight measurements without telling you if they were 5'3" or 6'3" tall. Numbers are meaningless without context, and understanding the *why* behind the numbers is often as powerful as the numbers themselves. You can save resources and reach your social sector destiny faster by prioritizing the development of your data stories. Being mindful of all the interconnected variables at play can unlock previously undiscovered, disregarded, or underappreciated pathways to progress.

The Power of the Hero's Journal

In *Indiana Jones and The Last Crusade*, Indiana embarks on a mission to rescue his father after learning of his capture by Nazis while on a quest to find the Holy Grail. Before his capture, Dr. Jones Sr. finds out his expedition partner is a Nazi and he promptly mails Indiana his diary for safekeeping. Why? The diary contains Dr. Jones Sr.'s lifelong research on reaching the Holy Grail — including notes, illustrations, a map, and clues about how to overcome obstacles. It's important that the Nazis not get their hands on the diary, as they plan to use the Grail to achieve world domination. With the help of the diary, Indiana is able to recover his father, find the Holy Grail, and ultimately save the world from authoritarian rule.

Indiana's story reinforces the power of the "journey journal." Every adventurer should constantly be researching, documenting, and reflecting on their progress in a journey journal if they want to maintain momentum towards their Holy Grail. While Dr. Jones Sr. wasn't able to find the Holy Grail by himself, his research — compiled in his Holy Grail diary — is what led directly to his rescue and to the father-son pair eventually finding the coveted chalice. Why does this matter? Journey journals don't exist purely for the journaler's benefit. Their real magic is in helping others in similar situations overcome obstacles on the path to their destiny. Journey journals are communication tools that help others and our future selves understand what worked, what we may have gotten wrong, and what obstacles we have yet to overcome.

Journey journaling isn't just a fun idea restricted to the realm of fantasy. Funders and grantees can create their own journey journals to help themselves, their colleagues, and their communities better understand themselves and their data to make better decisions. As it usually takes the form of a research-based narrative, Results-Based Accountability's "Story Behind the Curve" (the second step in the Turn the Curve Thinking) can serve as a journey journal to help you and your partners understand the factors that are influencing the current state of your data. This increased understanding will allow you to create Action Plans with a higher likelihood of success, communicate your data with the world, and make better investment decisions.

The Story Behind the Curve — the Window to Discovery

Story Behind the Curve = a transparent analysis of the contributing and limiting factors that influence a data trendline's history and forecast for an Indicator or Performance Measure.

Data without context is relatively meaningless. Looking at your Indicators or Performance Measures without the Story Behind the Curve would be like taking all the material out of this book except the various metrics I've mentioned. This is just a guess, but I'm thinking that would leave about five pages of statistics. Maybe you'd be able to make some assumptions about what it all meant, but you wouldn't know why I wanted you to know those numbers or what to do next. The power of the numbers I've shared with you is their contextual position in a grander narrative — that of realizing your social sector destiny.

Good investment decisions rely on a deep understanding of the multivariate nature of reality. And community wellbeing and programmatic performance are highly multivariate. There are a plethora of variables that influence an Indicator or Performance Measure, and the more factors you can identify, the more sound your decision-making will be.

As often as possible, make sure you have a 'Story Behind the Curve' for each of your Indicators. A Story Behind the Curve explores contributing factors (reasons the data looks the way it does) and limiting factors (reasons preventing the data from getting better). Additionally, you should never ever ask your grantees to report on Performance Measures without a story.

What can go wrong if there's no story? One of the biggest mistakes is misinterpreting your grantees' data. One of your funded partners could have had a heroic performance in spite of external factors (like COVID, the economy, etc.). But without the analysis, you might just see a performance trendline going down over the past couple of years. What's likely to happen? You might cut their funding. If you're looking at numbers with no context, you won't know the difference between truly good performance or truly bad performance. Your grantee also won't understand their role in your larger story of impact if you don't provide Indicator stories.

Why should you document your Story Behind the Curve, instead of just thinking or talking about it? Documentation achieves transparency because it:

1. Provides a consistent insight on the evolving reasons for the state of the data that anyone can see

2. Demonstrates your thinking process to make your reasoning more accessible to others

3. Allows you to reference iterations of the Story Behind the Curve throughout time to see how things have changed.

It's one thing to be transparent in reporting data, but it's another thing to be open about how you think about the data. Documenting your thinking process allows others to join you in understanding what's going on and allows you to surface and challenge assumptions in a healthy way. For example, someone may read your Story Behind the Curve for "High school graduation rate" and say, "Here you mention that a limiting factor is that kids skip school because they find it boring, but in talking with a lot of local students, we've found that a large percentage of them say they're skipping because they feel unsafe at school." These two scenarios have very different implications for what will work to improve graduation rates.

The Nuts and Bolts of a Good Story Behind the Curve

Any effective Story Behind the Curve does the following four things:

1. Lists and explains contributing factors

2. Lists and explains limiting factors

3. Pursues and proposes research on root causes where appropriate

4. Surfaces and challenges assumptions

Approaching your story with a bulleted list of contributing and limiting factors is a time-effective way to get started and allows you to get more potential factors onto the table. Remember, you can always come back later and add a narrative. Let's discuss each of the four components above in more detail.

1. List and Explain Contributing Factors

Contributing factors explain why your data might be trending positively. If your data is trending in the wrong direction, contributing factors explain why the data isn't as bad as it could've been (i.e., the data could've been worse if we hadn't done X). Contributing factors focus on the positives or what's going well. Why start here? I've found that most people tend to focus on fixing the negatives and forget about maximizing the positives. But in many cases, replicating positive factors creates a positive feedback loop of greater impact.

Here's an example. Let's consider contributing factors for the "Percentage of children entering school ready to learn." Generally speaking, some contributing factors might include:

- Babies are being born healthy in that community
- There were prenatal screenings before the babies were born healthy
- There were home visits in that community before children entered school
- Many parents have access to quality, affordable childcare
- Most homes have parents who enjoy reading and reading to their children

2. List and Explain Limiting Factors

Limiting factors are the negative factors holding your data trendline back. I like to imagine limiting factors as the data troll from Chapter Five pulling the trendline the wrong direction. If your data is trending in the right direction, limiting factors are what's preventing the data from improving with an increasing level of acceleration. Using the same analogy of "Children entering school ready to learn," we could invert the contributing factors and turn them into limiting factors:

- Babies aren't being born as healthy as they could be
- There is a lack of prenatal screenings being performed
- There are no home visits prior to children entering school
- Parents have a lack of access to quality, affordable childcare

- Children aren't being read to at an early age.

When considering limiting factors, it's prudent to disaggregate your data. Oftentimes, you won't be able to figure out what's holding the data back until you disaggregate by race or the other systemic factors listed in Chapter Four.

3. Pursue and Propose Research on Root Causes Where Appropriate

While exploring contributing and limiting factors, you may find that more research is needed to understand the story behind the data. There's always going to be information you won't have at a certain point in time. Come up with a list of the information you still need, as this will ultimately allow you to identify a research agenda — actions that people need to take to further develop the Story Behind the Curve.

Let's say you're looking at the metric, "Percentage of people that live within walking distance of a playground or a safe space in their community." To understand the current level of access, you may need to find out exactly how many people or how many households live within walking distance of a particular park. Or, you might need to dig deeper and disaggregate the metric by race. This research can help you understand whether certain neighborhoods have fewer parks, thus directing the development of new parks where they're needed most. Ideally, you should assign one person to do this research between now and your next data check-in. Next time, you'll have a more informed and actionable discussion.

4. Surface and Challenge Assumptions

Wrong assumptions can be disastrous when they're the basis for any decision-making process that influences a large number of people. There are innumerable examples of faulty assumptions driving scientific research, policymaking, and budgeting. Take the Flat Earth Theory. Most people once assumed that Earth was flat and also the center of the universe. Today, we're highly technologically advanced, but imagine if scientists had understood the true nature of our solar system from the beginning. The fields of math, physics, and engineering would be light-years ahead of where they are now. Who knows what strange devices we'd have access to (or planets we'd be landing on) by now if we hadn't started with such an inaccurate assumption.

It's terrible that so many people throughout history have faced ridicule (at best) and persecution (at worst) for challenging wrong assumptions. Now, our success relies on making space for brave people who have different ways of thinking, experiences, and knowledge. Seek out people to join your social sector roundtable who can say, "No, I think you're wrong, and here's the evidence I have to prove it." These people are invaluable catalysts in the pursuit of social sector impact. We must risk feeling uncomfortable with new ideas in order to achieve progress. Try not to hold your assumptions too dear to your heart when developing your Story Behind the Curve. And use meetings with grantees to create healthy dialogue around surfacing and challenging assumptions.

Hero's Journey Spotlight: Connecticut Department of Children and Families

Anne McIntyre-Lahner has worked in the human services field for more than 40 years, including 26 years with the State of Connecticut, where she has served in numerous management roles for the Judicial Branch and the Department of Children and Families (DCF). Throughout her career, she has focused on systems change by developing and overseeing accountability practices and leading strategic planning and performance management work.

In 2016, Clear Impact's champion for children, Karen Finn, partnered with Anne to deliver the *Implementing RBA in the Children and Family Sector* webinar. In it they discuss the incredible impact RBA had on the department's decision-making, as well as notable Turned Curves like increasing the "Percentage of children in kinship care." At the time,

DCF focused on five mandated areas: child protective services, children's behavioral health, education for children in its care, prevention, and shared responsibility for the state's juvenile justice system. They operated out of one main office and 14 local offices, organized into six regions. To achieve impact, DCF contracted around 100 types of programs that served 36,000 children and 16,000 families.

At DCF, Anne implemented agency-wide utilization of Results-Based Accountability for internal and contracted-service planning and performance management, and implemented an outcome-focused approach in disaster-preparedness planning for the agency. She was a leader in Connecticut's inter-agency RBA projects. Now, as a certified RBA trainer, she regularly helps colleagues and service providers focus on results to improve their operations and outcomes. Most recently, Anne developed Action2Outcomes to support and empower government and nonprofit leaders who are ready to focus on outcomes.

After decades in the human services field, Anne knows how hard nonprofit and government employees work. She also knows how frustrating it can be to work really hard and still feel like you are just "spinning your wheels." That's why Anne is a huge advocate of the Results-Based Accountability Turn the Curve Process. Throughout her career, Anne realized that Stories Behind the Curve were instrumental in preventing impactful programs from getting cut by DCF.

Once, Anne had the opportunity to listen in as an agency told the Story behind a "poorly performing program." Due to understaffing, the program was unable to achieve one of the primary outcomes, an outcome that would result in participants being better off *and* lead to reimbursement for some program costs. The grantee's Story Behind the Curve helped various funders understand that, in order to improve performance, the program in question truly needed increased staff resources to deliver services in a way that would ensure participants were better off after participation, and lead to the program being able to generate increased revenue.

Anne describes the Story Behind the Curve as an opportunity to talk about "the good, the bad, and the ugly." It is an opportunity to increase everybody's understanding of performance by identifying the forces at work that impact the program or effort that is being reported. According to Anne, "The story behind the baseline... provides the context for the reader to fully understand the performance, and it empowers the practitioners to understand the necessary actions to turn the curve on performance."

Anne invites fellow Social Sector Heroes to consider the following examples of forces that may be part of your story:

1. Forces can be internal to an agency, like internal communication. For example, co-workers may not understand how to make referrals for service, resulting in low utilization. There may also be positive or negative staffing impacts.

2. Forces can also be external to an agency. These can include forces as large as the economy — for example, there may be low hiring rates for trainees competing for jobs with experienced workers who have been laid off. Even the weather, which is out of the practitioner's control, may have an effect — such as poor attendance at parenting classes due to multiple snowstorms. External forces can also be as direct as relationships with referral agencies or the need for system training.

Additionally, Anne says it's "important *not* to rehash the data" in the Story Behind the Curve — the data graph has already provided that information. Instead, you should provide the most important contextual information to make sense of the data. Some questions you can ask to drive Story Behind the Curve conversations include:

-   Is the program performing as anticipated?
-   What has happened so far?

- Who are the partners in the effort and how do they relate with each other?

- What is the climate in which you are operating?

- What positively impacted performance?

- What negatively impacted performance?

- How does this story inform your understanding of your performance?

- How can it inform your efforts to Turn the Curve?

Understanding data stories, in conjunction with performance data, helped Anne and Connecticut DCF identify where to focus their attention and effort to improve community outcomes and improve their ROI through effective social investing. Specifically, staff were able to utilize the data narratives to identify the actions needed to improve performance, modify the approach to the service (or the effort needed to include those actions), implement them, and measure their impact. One major success included increasing the "Percentage of children in kinship care" (children in the care of a blood relative) by around 20 percentage points from 2011 to 2016. You can learn more about this effort at SocialSectorHero.com/Resources.

Connecticut DCF currently shares their data stories in CT Kids Report Card Scorecards hosted publicly on their website. The Scorecards contain Indicator Data measuring progress towards the achievement of the CT Result, "All Connecticut children grow up in a stable living environment, safe, healthy, and prepared to lead successful lives." Connecticut has one of the best efforts around including Stories Behind the Curve that I've ever seen. In more cases than not, each Indicator is presented with a narrative to help viewers contextualize the data. You can view these Scorecards at SocialSectorHero.com/Resources.

Diversity in Perspective

In *The Lord of the Rings*, the fellowship tasked with delivering the One Ring to Mordor is incredibly diverse. There are Hobbits, an elf, a Dwarf, a wizard, and multiple humans — all with diverse skills, weapons abilities, backgrounds, and knowledge. The fellowship even gets help from trees, horses, and various other animals along the way. It doesn't get more diverse than that. If you imagine your own favorite tale of adventure, I guarantee it's filled with all kinds of beings. Why? No quest is possible without diversity. An important part of a hero's development occurs when they realize they can't do it alone and they don't have all the answers.

Besides being a fan of fantastical tales of heroism, I'm also a proponent of approaching the work of social sector impact through a lens of Diversity, Equity, and Inclusion. While authentic DEI is about much more than hiring a bunch of different people of different races, it is an important first step. A diverse workforce helps improve everything from employee productivity, morale, decision-making, business outcomes, and finances.

Non-diverse leadership teams make faster decisions, but they may not make the most effective decisions. Diversity may sometimes mean slower decision-making, but this time investment is worth it. There is a large body of evidence showing that diversity leads to better financial outcomes and operational productivity. According to McKinsey & Company, gender-diverse companies are 15 percent more likely to financially outperform those that aren't and ethnically-diverse companies are 35 percent more likely to outperform those that aren't (both of these statistics are noted in Clear Impact's *DEI Made Measurable* ebook, which you can find at SocialSectorHero.com/Resources).

Diversity in internal decision-making doesn't just benefit the forprofit world. It also serves an important role in creating your data stories. The more people you involve in constructing your Story Behind the Curve, the more illuminating, compelling, and actionable the story will become. It's important to solicit diverse perspectives and ideas when identifying root causes and challenging assumptions. Your understanding and strategies are almost guaranteed to improve. Staff, funded partners, and community leaders are some of the obvious groups you'll want to engage. Within these groups, ensure there is appropriate representation in race, gender, age, and any other variable that's important to you.

I've been part of Story Behind the Curve discussions with groups of two people and groups of 200 people. Size doesn't really matter here. It's important to keep in mind, however, that the larger your social sector fellowship becomes, the more important it will be for you to find expert facilitation. When seeking facilitators for your Story behind the Curve discussions, be sure the individual is adept at managing diverse viewpoints and potentially heated discussions.

A Simple Process to Develop Your Stories

Hopefully, you now understand the elements that make up an actionable Story Behind the Curve. But you might be thinking, "How do I actually develop the story?" Lucky for you, there's a simple four-step process that I — and many of our Clear Impact consultants — have successfully implemented with clients around the globe. This process is so effective because it allows for all personality types to participate (again, supporting diversity). In this process there will ideally be a large group that you break up into smaller groups.

Step 1: Brainstorming

First, break up your large group into several smaller groups. In each small group, each person should write down what they think are the most important factors on a particular trendline. Once you've done that for about five minutes, ask each person to share their ideas with the small group as a whole and have them discuss. This way, everyone's talking and participating. During the discussion, have someone document each idea on a flip chart or on a screen to enhance understanding with a visual. Make sure everyone's ideas are captured accurately. All ideas are good ideas at this point.

Step 2: Passionate Selling

Next, within each small group, ask each person to "passionately sell" what they perceive to be the most important contributing and limiting factor to the larger group. Passionate selling is just a fancy way of saying "convincing people to get on board with your way of thinking." It's like being a salesperson for an idea. Give each salesperson no more than 30-45 seconds to make their case, and make sure everyone gets the same amount of time. Each person can pick a different factor or the same factor as someone else.

Step 3: Vote

After listening to each passionate selling presentation, give each person in the smaller group an opportunity to vote on the top three factors. Each person can get up and physically put sticky dots on their flip chart of choice or the facilitator can read the ideas out loud and people raise their hands for their favorite. Once you've got your priority list based on the voting, you can give the entire group a chance to comment and refine the list further based on the ensuing discussion.

Step 4: Share with the Larger Group

Each group then shares their top three ideas from the voting with the larger group. Look for common themes and energy from the larger group around the most important factors. Try to organize these into two different lists — contributing factors and limiting factors — impacting the trend. If the common themes are not abundantly clear, and there is a need to seek consensus or get further clarity on the perspective of the larger group, give everyone an opportunity again to vote on their top two factors in each category. From there, it should be the prerogative of the convener to decide how to make the final call on what is included.

Step 5: Do it All Again

The purpose of this exercise isn't to do it one time and have the list of factors be set in stone forever. Make it an iterative process and refine your list of factors on a regular basis as you learn new information.

Hero's Journey Spotlight: Berkshire United Way

Pittsfield is the largest city and seat of Berkshire County, Massachusetts. Like many New England manufacturing centers, it experienced a significant economic decline in the latter part of the twentieth century. However, with environmental initiatives, industrial property reconstruction, and growth in arts and entertainment, the city has redefined itself as a cultural and economic powerhouse. Forbes ranked Pittsfield as number 61 in its 2006 list of Best Small Places for Business. In 2009, Massachusetts chose the city to receive a 2009 Commonwealth Award, the state's highest award in the arts, humanities, and sciences.

Pittsfield is also home to Berkshire United Way (BUW). Berkshire United Way is helping children, families, and individuals learn and grow, make smart decisions, and find stability in life by supporting programs that focus on early childhood development, positive youth development, and economic prosperity. Through Community Impact work in Fiscal Year 2021, BUW was able to help 13,443 individuals in 38 programs across 25 agencies.

Despite the city's accolades, there's a different side of the city and county. As of 2020, the percentage of Berkshire children who score at or above proficient on Grade 3 MCAS English tests is down from the last 10 years and is lower than the state average. High school graduates planning for college have also seen a decline, likely due to the COVID-19 pandemic. Median household income saw an increase, but it was still significantly lower than the state average in 2020, and the gap continued to grow. Due to this troubling data, BUW is focusing on improving third-grade literacy, high-schoolers planning for post-secondary education, and median household income.

BUW was already concerned about these issues nearly a decade before they really came to light. In order to make a serious impact on their focus areas, Social Sector Heroes at BUW realized in 2013 they needed a way to track their community partners' outcomes. This prompted them to seek training in several social impact frameworks. Prior to 2013, BUW had already adopted Collective Impact, Results-Based Accountability, and Asset Based Community Development and had integrated them into their internal strategic plan. Colleagues from one of BUW's sister organizations, United Way of Central Iowa, had recently visited and shared their experience of using Clear Impact consultants and software to build their outcomes tracking systems. Julie Singley, BUW's Coordinator of Research and Evaluation at the time, was all in. She looped in Dan Duncan, one of Clear Impact's Senior Consultants, to facilitate community training and work with them to develop their strategic planning process.

During the design phase of their new outcomes measurement initiative, a BUW implementation team worked closely with Clear Impact staff. The team utilized the Clear Impact Scorecard to set up data dashboards to monitor and improve progress across their entire fellowship. On the Population Accountability front, they set up dashboards for each of their three focus areas and each corresponding Strategy for each partner agency to report programmatic outcomes (home visiting, quality early education and care, mentoring, career readiness, etc.).

Understanding the importance of journaling their impact story, BUW also ensured partners provided a Story Behind the Curve, a list of partners, ideas on What Works, and an Action Plan for each target performance measure. To get the most out of the software, the implementation team attended Scorecard University and worked closely with several team members at Clear Impact to learn more about implementing Scorecard effectively. By July of 2017, all community partners were using Scorecard to measure performance.

Why did BUW find Clear Impact Scorecard so valuable? Notably, it helps their partners to journal their impact journey and document answers to essential RBA questions. While she was still with the organization in 2019, Singley shared that, "We highly value the Clear Impact Scorecard system that helps us aggregate all of our community partner work as well as it's able to capture both quantitative as well as qualitative data. So, our partners can share the Story Behind the Curve and explain why the data is looking the way it does."

Some of the benefits BUW experienced as a result of their new initiatives included:

- Funded partners were easily able to share their success with other funders

- BUW could more easily see trends and aggregate/disaggregate data by focus area/strategy

- Early childhood partners began consistently performing well

- BUW engages in more effective data-based decision-making, funding, and communication.

You can read the full list of benefits in Clear Impact's official BUW Scorecard Case Study at SocialSectorHero.com/Resources.

To BUW, community impact isn't just a process for making investment decisions. It's the endgame. That endgame includes literate children that grow up into happy, healthy, educated youth, literate adults and financially stable people — the keys to a good life. By directing resources to programs and initiatives that meet the broad range of needs in these areas, they create sustainable change. Ultimately, RBA and Scorecard are helping BUW to see whether they are making measurable progress towards these end goals.

Having already established accountability and impact measurement systems, BUW would've undoubtedly made progress on its focus areas. But the entire effort was accelerated through the three key tools mentioned in this chapter: RBA's Turn the Curve Process (particularly the Story Behind the Curve), the Clear Impact Scorecard's qualitative data analysis functionality (Story Behind the Curve reporting), and the help of expert facilitation from champions for change like Dan Duncan.

CHAPTER 7 ACTION PLAN

1. If you're focused on a Population Indicator, gather a diverse set of community leaders to help you develop a Story Behind the Curve, utilizing the exercise laid out in this chapter. The more diversity within the group the better. If you're focused on a Performance Measure for your organization, gather a handful of staff. All forms of diversity are also important here, including levels within the organization.

2. Research professional facilitators who can help you. This can often allow all participants to be equal participants in creating the Story Behind the Curve. Clear Impact has several full-time professional facilitators and trainers. Contact us at Info@ClearImpact.com to see if any would be a good fit for your efforts.

3. Optional: Read *Stop Spinning Your Wheels — Using Results-Based Accountability to Steer Your Agency to Success* by Anne McIntyre-Lahner. This is a quick, interesting read that talks more about RBA Implementation at the Connecticut Department of Children and Families. You can find it at SocialSectorHero.com/Resources.

CHAPTER 8:
ASSEMBLE THE ALLIES
(SUPPORT EFFECTIVE DIALOGUE)

"The single biggest problem in communication is the illusion that it has taken place." – George Bernard Shaw

My oldest son Connor started sixth grade in the midst of COVID-19. Due to the circumstances, he would have to attend school and complete his assignments virtually. Connor loves school and has a fierce appetite for learning. He always does his best and gets good grades no matter what life seems to throw at him. Because he holds himself accountable, we got used to not having to worry about pushing him. When he started sixth grade, we assumed things would stay the same. Virtual school seemed a lot more flexible. But it wasn't that simple.

Not only did Connor have to make the normal adjustments a child has to make when transitioning from elementary to middle school, but he had to do it while learning from home in the midst of a pandemic. Online schooling adds another layer of complexity — you have to learn *how to learn online* effectively if you want to maintain the same level of achievement. Online learning introduces so many questions. Is it harder to pay attention to someone in virtual class than it is face-to-face? What are the solutions for that? How can you limit distractions when your entire family is at home? What do you do if you're having technical difficulties? What role do non-academic activities play in the learning process (recess, talking to friends, walking to class)? The list goes on and on.

Let's just say Connor's first midterm report card wasn't what we all expected — himself included. If we just jumped down his throat after looking at his grades, it would not have been a productive conversation. But by having a psychologically safe and open conversation with him, we were able to figure out what was holding him back from doing his best. For one, interactions between students and teachers are more restricted. It's not as easy to just walk up to the teacher's desk after class and ask clarifying questions. Once a Zoom meeting ends, the connection is severed and you have to rely on phone calls and emails, so it takes much longer to get a response.

Due to some of these communication issues, Connor had misinterpreted that some of his assignments were optional. He was either handing them in late and getting partial credit or missing them completely. He was also having difficulty uploading his assignments. All of us were also unaware that we could track assignment completion and grades via the school's online learning platform. This was an important part of the story because accessing previously graded assignments is an important part of Connor's ability to improve his work over time.

Grades do not equal effort and data does not equal good or bad performance. If we had only judged Connor's midterm performance using the grades alone (data with no context), our solutions would've been based on faulty assumptions. And to obtain the relevant context, we had to have an effective dialogue with Connor and create a space where he felt comfortable being honest and that we were allies in his success. After talking about it for a while, we got clarity on what questions needed answering and what actions we could take to help Connor do better. Our first step was to explore the assignment portal, get clearer instructions from teachers, and help Connor learn how to use it properly. Since then, he hasn't had any more issues and has gotten straight As.

Grades are like performance data for a student or group of students. In a way, your grantees' Performance Measures are their grades. Similar to our middle school saga, you should create a space for your partners and grantees to tell you the stories behind their measures. You must seek to understand what is going on before jumping to conclusions or taking drastic actions. The best way to do this is to approach conversations from a place of fellowship (everyone is an ally on the social impact journey with valuable talents, knowledge, perspectives, and resources).

What Does it Take to Seize the Sword?

In this chapter, we've reached a pivotal point in your Social Sector Hero's journey. All the previous steps we've covered are important, but they mean nothing if you cannot communicate effectively with your staff and funded partners. Navigating communication pitfalls effectively and taking advantage of opportunities for increased understanding will help you avoid stalled progress due to unproductive conversations.

The framework of the traditional hero's journey story is sometimes referred to as the "Monomyth" and consists of 12 steps.[45] Artists throughout time and space have created the most beloved hero's stories based on this framework. Perhaps the most exciting and important stages occur in the moments leading up to and ending with the hero "seizing the sword" — taking possession of the object of their quest (love, treasure, saving the world, knowledge, a magical sword, reconciliation, etc.). Your sword(s) might be things like social impact, Turned Curves, equitable outcomes,

---

45 https://libguides.gvsu.edu/c.php?g=948085&p=6857311#:~:text=The%20
Hero%27s%20Journey%20is%20a,Finally%20is%20the%20return

community wellbeing, or specific data targets. Regardless, there are several things that must happen before any hero can seize their sword.

First, a Social Sector Hero approaches "The Innermost Cave." The Innermost Cave is usually represented as a physically or psychologically perilous place, in which the object of the quest is hidden. This is because the best and most valuable things in life take immense effort to get. To reach the object, you must first learn how to navigate The Innermost Cave effectively to avoid or overcome danger. Next, you and your allies (partners) must utilize all you've learned along your journey to face and overcome the danger in the cave — this is the "Supreme Ordeal." Finally, if you are successful, you'll seize your sword.

You're probably not going to approach any physical danger in your quest for social impact. But there are symbolically dangerous pitfalls you can stumble into if you're not careful. Remember the havoc wreaked by the data troll's antics — not disaggregating data, not including the Story Behind the Curve, and cutting budgets based on numbers alone. While you won't have to worry about physical harm, these pitfalls can metaphorically "kill" your progress if you're not prepared.

To navigate these pitfalls and get closer to capturing the object of your quest, the most important tool you have at your disposal is effective dialogue. Effective dialogue with your allies will prepare you for the next stages of your journey, including the on-the-ground work, action-plan management, and continual alteration of plans to obtain measurable progress. Effective dialogue increases your odds of seizing the sword and achieving what you set out to do.

What is Effective Dialogue?

Effective Dialogue = communicative actions, guided by effective questions and deep listening, among two or more parties that results in both parties understanding each other and taking action.

While writing this book, I had a really good conversation with our company's Executive Vice President, Justin Miklas, about roles and expectations. By letting him lay out how he understands his role and expectations (for him and for me), it allowed us to ask better questions about time management and capacity issues. This understanding informed our strategy for change, including what work could be delegated. By seeking to understand context first instead of just assuming we were right, we figured out mutually beneficial ways to save time and advance the company's goals.

Effective dialogue consists of communicative actions between two or more parties that result in both parties understanding each other's ideas. This includes understanding contributions to the Common Purpose, the state of the data, Stories Behind the Curve, Strategies, Action Plans, and the rationale behind each. Effective dialogue occurs face-to-face (in person or virtual) and requires diverse groups to have opportunities to participate, speak their minds, and challenge assumptions. To do this, there must be mutual respect and above-average trust.

Exploring grantee Turn the Curve Plans in depth is a great way to practice creating conditions for effective dialogue. Program and grant leaders will not just think it is a paper exercise if the data, story, and plan are the basis for a conversation on a regular basis with their boss or funder. Turn the Curve meetings aren't the end-all-be-all, but they allow for diverse parties to surface and challenge assumptions where differences in perspectives matter most. Allowing your grantees to outline and share their thinking before you meet face-to-face will allow you to formulate useful, non-leading questions (i.e. questions that don't prompt a particular response).

At the end of effective dialogue, there should be a common understanding of everyone's next steps. Concluding every conversation with an Action Plan or next steps creates a clear sense of what needs to happen next, when, and by whom. If you do this well, your dialogues will result in an enhanced level of trust, commitment to the Common Purpose, more accurate data, and accountability for action.

Vanquish Fear of the Data Monster

Effective communication is important in any relationship. Moving beyond the pleasantness of conversations, it can maximize performance for you and your grantees. One of the biggest obstacles holding us back from having effective dialogues about performance, accountability, and data, is the fear of the data troll's cousin — the 'data monster.' The data monster is the physical manifestation of the fear of repercussions due to "bad" performance. This justifiable fear stems from a history of punitive budgetary action from funders on data with no context.

One of a grantee's biggest worries is that you will cut their funding due to temporary setbacks. This may cause them to hide from performance conversations. It's not just about losing funding, but a fear of being perceived as bad at managing the grant. Funders can help vanquish the data monster by creating effective dialogues that uncover the context and treat the grantee as an ally in the journey to measurable impact. Center your conversations around driving continual improvement — not meting out punishment as soon as the data falls beneath an arbitrary threshold. Assure your grantees that you won't abandon them at the first sign of conflict but will instead use setbacks as learning opportunities to move forward on the journey to social impact together.

If handled appropriately, your grantees should come to view dialogue around their performance as a tool to fulfill the Common Purpose. You can also view it as a tool to optimize and protect your investments. When you design your questions about a grantee's data in a way that reinforces a desire to understand their unique story and challenges, both parties can then join together in developing corrective actions. This will create a collaborative dynamic that reinforces the Common Purpose and continued accountability for action.

Hero's Journey Spotlight: United Way of Central Iowa

United Way of Central Iowa (UWCI) is part of a special group of United Ways raising $25 million or more annually. They also fund over 150 programs per year. The city it calls home — Des Moines, Iowa — is the number one city for per capita United Way giving among people who are employed. To create impact, UWCI aligns nonprofits, businesses, governments, and community leaders to implement collaborative strategies aimed at improving the five elements of a thriving community (Economic Opportunity, Education Success, Early Childhood Success, Essential Needs, and Health and Well-Being).

UWCI staff learned about Results-Based Accountability in the 1990s after being funded by the Annie E. Casey Foundation as a new "Making Connections" site — "a collaboration of local organizations and residents that seeks to improve outcomes for disadvantaged children by strengthening their families, improving their neighborhoods, and raising the quality of local services."[46]

UWCI saw the value of RBA because of its ability to democratize the data. Democratizing data involves gathering complex systems-level data (like low birthweight rates and high school graduation rates), using the distillation process, and presenting it in simpler, visual ways like charts, maps, and graphs. This allows program staff and community residents to more easily understand the data. Democratization empowered various groups to engage in collective discussions with the shared knowledge that neighborhoods, communities, and even individual citizens could play key roles in solving complex community issues. United Way of Central Iowa was then able to pivot to the Community Impact framework proposed by United Way Worldwide because of their relationship with the Annie E.

---

46 https://mcstudy.norc.org/#:~:text=The%20Making%20Connections%20initiative%2C%20funded,the%20quality%20of%20local%20services.

Casey Foundation and the RBA framework. Since the early 2000s, UWCI has used RBA as the framework to drive its strategic planning, improve the quality of life for all people in Central Iowa, and improve the performance of funded programs.

Numerous Social Sector Heroes have called UWCI home over the years. Some of them include Shannon Cofield (President when RBA was adopted), Elisabeth Buck (former President), and Mary Sellers (current President).

Back in 2010, there was a driving force to measure UWCI's aggregate impact through a Unified Data Management System for funded partners to report performance. I still remember visiting Des Moines in January 2010 for our software kickoff meetings. Considering there was three feet of snow when I was there, I think I picked the wrong time to visit. Anyway, I am proud to say that over the course of our partnership, UWCI has built a model performance reporting system. After the launch, each UWCI grantee had to submit data on a few consistent but flexible Performance Measures. Additionally, they got to choose one measure for which to complete a Turn the Curve Plan to support meaningful dialogue. Years later, UWCI discovered an added value of their data system, as it is used to aggregate data entered into United Way Worldwide's Global Results Framework scorecards.

Ever since then (excluding COVID-19), UWCI staff and volunteer evaluators have met face-to-face with each grantee to ask questions about the stories behind their plans. Three to five volunteers and a few staff members score the plans to evaluate and support past and future investment decisions. They also ensure that staff and volunteers consider staffing challenges and other factors influencing differences in the quality of the writing. They understand that just because one organization doesn't have the resources for a professional writer, it doesn't mean they aren't doing good work. These conversations are helpful because they allow UWCI to look beyond the numbers and surface information not included in grantees' written narratives.

When it comes to improving educational success through effective communication, UWCI shines bright. Before 2009, UWCI was funding a lot of education programs, but the individual programs, if tracking performance data at all, were only collecting data relevant to their own missions. Many weren't tracking performance at all. All of this changed when UWCI set the community's Goals for 2020. In so doing, UWCI helped shift the focus to one of its goals (high school graduation), and created a framework to collectively improve that goal through effective programming and reporting, relying on similar data points across multiple agencies.

When UWCI started creating their Story Behind the Curve for high school graduation, effective dialogue with high schoolers was instrumental. Part of the research involved asking open-ended questions to find out why teens were dropping out or were at risk of dropping out — instead of basing decisions on previous assumptions. As a result, UWCI came to better understand the barriers facing these teens, including the fact that many had to work to support their families. Some of them even had their own children to support. This data led the community to ask, "How do we help kids earn credit if they can't go to school Monday through Friday, 7:30am to 3:00pm?"

This line of questioning led to the establishment of a flexible credit recovery model including academic support labs where kids could come in on their own time and earn credit. In 2013, they expanded the program to include kids who were under-credited or who would otherwise struggle to graduate. At the same time, they conducted outreach to teens who were dropping out of school or who didn't show up, to try and re-engage them and get them to consider the academic support lab. The result? UWCI and their partners were able to improve their strategies based on the Story Behind the Curve. Des Moines Public School is the largest and most diverse school in central Iowa, serving over 31,000 students PK-12. From

2008 to 2014, Des Moines Public School's four-year high school graduation rate rose from 65.10 percent to 81.68 percent.

Consistent and effective dialogue focused on surfacing unique grantee challenges annually, along with addressing equity, has also led to other measurable improvements. UWCI heroes are proud that local businesses have been supportive of the effort for data-based decision-making, given that it's also how they operate in their decisions to grow, expand, or contract. Using common processes, methodologies, and language across the entire fellowship has helped streamline performance reporting and evaluation. What's their best advice stemming from years of RBA experimentation and implementation? When aggregating across like programs, let your tools do the math. It saves so much time to only have to set something up once.

UWCI must be doing something right because 57 percent of all target measures across their grantee portfolio are trending in the right direction as of 2022 — up five percent over the previous two years, despite the pandemic. How many funders do you know who can tell you what percentage of their grantees' most important measures are trending in the right direction *and* making improvements annually? According to UWCI's 2020 Community Impact report, over the past 10 years, the Central Iowa five-year graduation rate has improved from 83 percent to 94 percent.

More Trust = Better Dialogue

Trust is one of the most important factors influencing the funder/ grantee relationship. It enhances transparency, reinforces commitment to the Common Purpose, and maximizes results. Trust can also help create a sense of psychological safety for your staff and partners, which will lead to everyone doing their job more effectively and prevent you from losing progress as a result of turnover, conflict avoidance, and fear of data. Below, I'll briefly dive into the importance of psychological safety when it comes to supporting open communication with your partners. In the next chapter, I'll dive into the "trust factor" in more depth.

Effective dialogue is impossible unless people feel comfortable speaking up, or unless they have a strong sense of psychological safety. According to Harvard Business School professor, Amy Edmonson, 'psychological safety' is defined as a "shared belief held by members of a team that the team is safe for interpersonal risk-taking."[47] Furthermore, psychological safety is "a sense of confidence that the team will not embarrass, reject or punish someone for speaking up." People who feel psychologically safe are more likely to volunteer valuable input that can help improve decision-making. With a high level of psychological safety, people are more likely to admit mistakes, partner together, and take on new roles.

During a study of the attributes of its most successful teams, Google found psychological safety to be the number one predictor of a high-performing team, ahead of dependability, structure, clarity, meaning, and impact. They also found that psychological safety influenced every other important dimension of employee engagement and productivity. Google also found that teams with higher psychological safety were less likely to quit, more open to new ideas, brought in more revenue, and were rated twice as effective by executives.[48]

How do you create psychological safety? Whether you're engaging with your employees or grantees, make them feel like they're a part of critical organizational processes (help them see the connection to the Common Purpose). You must also actively embrace diverse people and their perspectives, accept differences, include employees in decisions surrounding their work, treat employees at all levels of your organization fairly, create an

---

47 https://www.nytimes.com/2016/02/28/magazine/what-google-learned-from-its-quest-to-build-the-perfect-team.html

48 https://rework.withgoogle.com/blog/five-keys-to-a-successful-google-team/

open and safe place to express ideas, and encourage positive relationships. Finally, be transparent about your thinking and never make decisions on data without the context. In some cases sharing that you're trying to be more transparent and want to build trusting relationships, and then asking your partners for their ideas on how to help you do so, can lead to higher levels of trust and psychological safety in and of itself.

You can learn more about the ideas in this section in our DEI ebook at SocialSectorHero.com/Resources.

Effective Dialogue from the Start

Introductory conversations with newly funded partners set the stage for continued trust, commitment, and accountability. They are pivotal for the success of both parties. In 2013, Caroline Altman Smith, Senior Program Officer at The Kresge Foundation shared tips with the Center for Effective Philanthropy on how to have productive conversations with grantees directly post-award. She drew this advice from CEP's Working Well With Grantees, released that year. These tips are awesome, so I'll briefly summarize my favorites below. For further learning, you can access the full list at SocialSectorHero.com/Resources.

1. Assign One Point-Person

Both the funder and the grantee should be clear on who they should be talking to (this should be the same two people every time).

2. In-Person Communication is Best

As much as possible, make conversations about critical information face-to-face (virtual counts). This will help you avoid "out of sight, out of mind" syndrome.

3. Make Reporting Requirements Clear From the Beginning

Make sure your grantee understands your reporting culture, structure, reporting templates, data management systems, and guidelines. This may include training around reporting software and grading rubrics (don't forget you can access a sample grading rubric for Turn the Curve conversations at SocialSectorHero.com/Resources.

4. Avoid Communication Droughts

Don't just make contact annually! This will make your relationship seem uncaring and transactional. Don't be afraid of informal contact to check-in but make sure both parties are aware of preferences and expectations.

5. Be Transparent with Difficult Information

Be proactive and transparent about anything that affects the relationship, including financial difficulties, staffing changes, or anything affecting program implementation.

Focus on Questions that Advance Your Quest

Whether you're hosting a 1x4 meeting for a particular measure or designing a Common Purpose, there are certain things that must occur for you to effectively navigate the "Innermost Cave" of communication and increase your chances of seizing your sword — social impact! A quick reminder: effective dialogue ideally results in alignment, agreement, accountability, and action.

Turn the Curve Plan development, reporting, and iteration is the first opportunity you should consider when improving your communication with grantees. To prepare for an effective dialogue, design at least one or two questions for each step in the process (the Story Behind the Curve, Partners, What Works, Strategies, and Action Plan). Coming prepared with your questions ahead of time will allow you to make the best use of your time and dig deeper. Ask questions before offering advice. And consider making your concluding question, "How can I, as the funder, help you achieve measurable improvement on your measures?"

Asking the right questions — and ensuring there are open-ended questions — allows your grantees to surface information, challenges, and needs you can address. For example, they may raise the need for a better data infrastructure. Additionally, some grantees may surface a desire for more flexibility with their funding or staffing. There are virtually endless ways to spend money in a way that gets results. One partner's spending might look very different from another. They might ask for more funds or other resources. Maybe they're interested in connecting with other grantees to collaborate. You'll never know any of this if you don't ask.

Effective Questions to Engage Grantees in Performance Improvement Dialogue

With over 30 years of experience helping top executives create focus and alignment to achieve results, Doug Krug is a true organization and cultural transformation expert. He has worked with numerous government funders including executive teams of the FBI, NASA, Medicare/Medicaid, the IRS, EPA, Secret Service, US Marshals, NOAA, the US Coast Guard, Governor's Cabinets, and law enforcement and security agencies. In 2008, Doug developed what he called 'effective questions' for successful leadership. According to Doug, effective questions are usually open-ended, focus on the positive, and foster action. Effective questions should create a sense of possibility while avoiding issues of blame that can trigger defensiveness.

Doug's guidelines for effective questions can also help you have better, more actionable dialogues with your grantees that get everyone aligned and making better decisions. I'll provide some samples of effective questions below, based on Doug's guidelines. You can read more about the benefits of effective questions and access more examples at SocialSectorHero. com/Resources. The next Hero's Journey spotlight will also serve as an example of an organization successfully using effective questions like these.

General Questions About the Grantee's Organization or Program:

1. What are your strengths?

2. What improvements have you made recently?

3. What have been the benefits of those improvements?

4. What areas of your performance please you most?

5. What specifically about your performance would you like to be recognized for?

Questions Focused on a Particular Grantee Performance Measure:

1. What would it look like if suddenly you could perform at [name a number or rate that would represent a dramatic improvement]?

2. Of everything that you do in this area of performance, what are the two or three things that contribute most to your success?

3. What can I do to help and truly support your efforts?

4. What other organizations do you know of, with similar clients and resources, that have been especially successful with respect to this performance measure?

Questions to Help you Move From Ends to Means (Indicators or Performance Measures)

1. How are you/we doing (with respect to the measure)?

2. What are the most important factors influencing the trend of the measure?

3. Who are key partners with a role to play in improving this measure?

4. What would work to improve it?

    a. Do the proposed actions address one or more of the root causes identified?

    b. Are the proposed actions evidence-based?

    c. What are some no-cost or low-cost options?

5. What do you/we propose to do to improve performance?

    a. How strongly will the proposed strategy or action impact the data?

    b. Is the proposed strategy or action feasible?

    c. What will be done, when, how, and by whom?

Questions That Might be Useful if the Grantee Identifies an Obstacle:

1. What options do you have for getting past the obstacle?

2. What has worked most effectively for you in similar situations?

3. Who else has been successful in addressing a similar obstacle?

Before meeting with grantees, your Project Officers should 1) conduct a preliminary analysis to identify what technical assistance or other resources would support the grantee's performance improvement, 2) develop your list of effective questions, and 3) provide your questions to the grantee ahead of time so they have time to do the research and thinking needed to provide useful and actionable information.

Hero's Journey Spotlight:
Health Resources and Services Administration,
Bureau of Primary Health Care

The Bureau of Primary Health Care (BPHC) is one bureau within the Health Resources and Services Administration (HRSA). HRSA is an agency of the U.S. Department of Health and Human Services. BPHC funds health centers in underserved communities so they can provide access to high-quality, affordable, patient-centered, comprehensive primary health care for nearly 29 million people who are low-income, uninsured, or face other obstacles to receiving health care. A little over 90 percent of the health center clients are at or below 200 percent of poverty and roughly two-thirds are racial and ethnic minorities. Health centers also serve 1.4 million homeless people and 400,000 veterans. All told, health centers serve 1 in 11 people in the US.

Social Sector Hero Jim Macrae has been at HRSA since 1992 and has led BPHC for more than 15 years. As head of BPHC, Jim manages a $5.7 billion budget that supports nearly 1,400 health centers operating approximately 14,000 health service delivery sites in every US state, the District of Columbia, Puerto Rico, the US Virgin Islands, and the Pacific Basin. Early on, as Associate Administrator, Jim and the BPHC staff decided to create some universal measures to better track the performance of its HRSA-supported health centers. They initially chose six clinical measures and three financial measures. The really powerful decision was in making these measures transparent to the health centers themselves and to the public. This transparency created a healthy competition among the health centers and pushed the entire health center community to improve. They also had the wisdom to disaggregate the data by race and ethnicity on health outcome measures from the beginning to assure a focus on health equity.

BPHC introduced Results-Based Accountability into the mix when they realized they needed a better way to engage grantees and create cultures that foster performance improvement. They wanted to transition from being a compliance-oriented grant-maker to a performance-oriented funder in service of improved health in underserved communities. They also wanted to enhance the skills of their roughly 160 program officers to more meaningfully engage with grantees around performance.

In 2008, Jim and BPHC contracted with Clear Impact to train all of the program officers in how to have effective conversations with grantees. The conversation guidelines were based on Turn the Curve planning; customized training and individualized coaching was provided to each of the Bureau's various branches. Training was also provided to BPHC contractors to reinforce the language and process of Results-Based Accountability.

In this process, it was important to engage the entire BPHC leadership team to embrace this new way of working and get their buy-in before rolling it out to staff. Some of these leaders included Cheryl Dammons, Associate Administrator at HRSA; Tracey Orloff, Director of Strategic Partnerships Division at BPHC, HRSA; Angela Powell, Office of Health Center Program Monitoring Director at BPHC, HRSA; Suma Nair, Director, Office of Quality Improvement at BPHC, HRSA who was important in setting up BPHC's unified data system for reporting; and Gina Capra, Senior Vice President at National Association of Community Health Centers.

BPHC integrated Results-Based Accountability concepts into their site visit guide and called it the "Program Analysis and Recommendations (PAR) Guiding Principles." The PAR Guiding Principles served as a comprehensive programmatic review tool for BPHC staff and health center grantees. It had three overall purposes:

1. To provide a rationale and record for grant decisions

2. To provide a history of the applicant's compliance and overall performance

3. To develop an Action Plan for working with health center grantees on compliance issues and/or performance improvement areas for the upcoming year.

Most importantly, the PAR Guiding Principles help BPHC Project Officers ask effective questions about grantee performance. The questions helped the Program Officer analyze the grantee's unique situation and review the key factors impacting their performance. They used this information to help health centers develop action plans to improve health outcomes and financial performance. One of the best things about the PAR Guiding Principles is that the questions were open-ended and were able to take the grantee's context into account. Project Officers then helped the grantee explore opportunities for improvement. Project Officers asked a series of questions to help both parties understand current performance and what it would take to improve (including strategies and technical assistance). You can access the full guide at SocialSectorHero.com/Resources.

As a result of the effective dialogue between Project Officers and grantees, HRSA reports that 79 percent of BPHC health centers have met or exceeded one of the Healthy People 2030 goals, a benchmark for national health goals while 50 percent met or exceeded five or more 2030 Healthy People goals. This success led to a push to have health centers recognized as patient-centered medical homes, and they have gone from 1 percent of health centers being accredited to now more than 77 percent. Most notably, from 2009 to 2020, blood pressure control of hypertensive patients has improved from 58 percent to 63.1 percent and early prenatal care of patients in the first trimester has increased from 67.3 percent to 73.5 percent. The increase in performance is massive when considering the sheer size of their patient pool.

Project Officers' analytical skills also significantly improved. Effective questions allowed BPHC to more easily gain insight into the root causes of performance data trends and tie strategies and actions back to these root causes. Program evaluation now happens annually in the application process and every three years in site visits. This has led to an overall 24 percent increase between 2007-2019 in customer satisfaction from grantees.

If you want to get better at communicating with and analyzing grantee performance to make effective decisions, Jim offers the following tips for any funder:

- Embrace having data and making it transparent
- Be OK with the good, the bad, and the ugly when looking at data
- Focus first on performance instead of compliance
- Support professional development for staff
- A focus on performance doesn't mean focusing on negative attributes. Focus on positive building blocks
- The key is asking the right questions and being inquisitive
- Focusing on the right questions is also more important than having all the answers as a leader in your organization.

CHAPTER 8 ACTION PLAN

1. Better prepare for your next meeting with grantees by designing a list of one or two questions you want to ask for each step
   in the Turn the Curve process:

   a. Consider the list of effective questions for grantees
      included in this chapter and select which ones you'd like
      to ask.

   b. Make sure there is at least one open-ended question
      towards the end of the discussion for partners to surface
      anything that's important to them.

   c. Make sure it's clear that grantees can challenge assump-
      tions, suggest new ideas, and ask you for more help.

CHAPTER 9:
A HERO FACES THE TRUTH
(REPORT YOUR DATA PUBLICLY)

"When you open the door toward openness and transparency, a lot of people will follow you through." – Kirsten Gillibrand

When I was fresh out of college in 2003, I was in a community leadership program called Impact Silver Spring. As a participant, I was required to identify a community need and create a project to address it. One of the needs I identified was that in East Silver Spring, Maryland — an area of high poverty — there were little to no opportunities for kids to participate in organized sports, especially those of immigrant families. With the help of a few friends, I created a nonprofit, Long Branch Athletic Association (LBAA), put together a board of directors, and started raising money. One of the barriers for our families was that parents were working multiple jobs and were unable to transport their kids to practices. To address this challenge, we began organizing teams, finding volunteer coaches, and coordinating rides to practices. Our project ended up serving thousands of kids with youth sports opportunities, mostly in soccer and basketball.

At the time, Steve Silverman was a county council member, a politician with big ambitions and even a bigger heart, who helped engage local businesses to make sizable donations to the project. We were also able to bring in community development block grant funding through the Montgomery County Government. One of the things that I decided to do, given my background in RBA, was to create a Turn the Curve plan on three programmatic Performance Measures and post them on the project website:

1. Number of children of low-income and immigrant families accessing a sports team

2. Number of volunteer coaching hours

3. Cost per child of low-income and immigrant families served

As far as I remember, nobody else in the nonprofit space was posting performance data online. Yet, here we were, a small nonprofit with a tiny budget, doing just that. I can tell you that almost every grant that we wrote, particularly for the county government, we won. And I think it really impressed the donors Steve Silverman was approaching. We'd say, "We know we are a very small nonprofit, but if you look at the public data, you can see that we're serving X number of kids and creating Y number of opportunities." In doing all of this, LBAA ended up raising close to half a million dollars over the five years that I was involved. This transparency with data made us highly successful for a new, unproven nonprofit.

I remember having a conversation with the Community Development Block Grant Manager for the county government — Stevens Brown. I met with him to talk about the application for funding and other ways that the county could support the project. He seemed immediately blown away by the fact that we even had performance data available, let alone displayed online. He even asked me to provide advice to other nonprofits to help them set up performance data web pages like ours.

I didn't realize it at the time, but the process of trying to get performance data onto a public website was pretty arduous. I was constantly creating Excel spreadsheets, cutting and pasting, coding them into the web page, and saving it. Then, a new cycle of data would come out and I had to do it all over again. It was clunky. It didn't look good. I wasn't a graphic designer, so it was pretty rudimentary. It did the job, but there was no "wow factor." This experience heavily influenced the creation of our Clear Impact Scorecard software back in 2010. I wanted to make things much easier than what I had to go through every month. Now, any time a user updates data in our system, it's automatically updated on their website (no copy-paste required!).

Alas, we didn't have access to something like Scorecard back in 2003. But because we were transparent with our data, we attracted attention: people could quickly understand what we were trying to achieve, what our impact was, and how our funding dollars translated into tangible, measurable results for children in the community. Impact Silver Spring — where it all started — was so impressed that they permanently adopted the program and brought it in-house. Today, Impact Sports still exists and serves hundreds of kids per year in the Long Branch, Wheaton, and Briggs Chaney neighborhoods of Montgomery County, MD.

Go Ahead — Stick Your Head in the Sand

Practicing Transparency = clearly communicating the state of wellbeing in your community, your performance data, your thinking and analysis, and your improvement plans in an easily accessible location, using plain language, and formatted for anyone to see and understand.

I'd like to tell you about a popular misconception about ostriches, if you'll stick with me for a moment. You may have heard it. At some point in time, some people saw ostriches submerging their heads in the sand and assumed they were hiding. Thus, "sticking your head in the sand" became an idiom for cowardice. But it turns out those folks got it all wrong! Ostriches can't fly, so they are unable to build their nests and lay their eggs in trees. To protect their brood from predators, they dig a hole in the ground, lay their eggs, and cover them with sand. Like those of any bird, eggs need heat to incubate. They need sunlight. So, the ostriches were never hiding — they were sticking their heads in the ground to rotate their eggs and ensure an even distribution of heat from the sun's rays. The lesson? We should all strive to be like the ostriches. Don't be afraid to dig down deep and bring your eggs — your data — to light, so that it can grow into something truly spectacular.

So, what is your ray of sunshine? What is your reward for bringing your data to light — and what happens if you don't? Well, publicly bringing light to your data creates transparency. Transparency requires that you clearly communicate your thinking, your performance, your community's wellbeing, your next steps, and how other people can help. Your just rewards will be greater alignment, urgency for your cause, public support, funding, and collaboration for results. If you aren't transparent, you may be perceived as secretive, misleading, or simply inept. At worst, your integrity may come into question. This can jeopardize your operations and potential impact.

Transparency is honestly communicating a piece of information regardless of what the piece of information contains — whether it's "good" or "bad." Think about any relationship where you felt you could trust the other person completely. Sharing information about your performance and impact (including the good, the bad, and the ugly) leads to more trust in your organization and your social sector fellowship as a whole. Transparency can help people see your true potential as a force for good and they'll be more likely to support you with their voices and dollars.

If people can quickly go to your website to see your 'eggs' — how you're doing on key Indicators and Performance Measures — there will be more of an impetus for them to reach out to support your impact journey. You'll stay competitive with donors, whether they're individuals, government agencies, businesses, or other funders. You'll also help attract more funding and support for your grantee's programs. According to a 2019 study, "Nonprofits that are more transparent and share things publicly, like audited financial reporting, goals, strategies, capabilities, and metrics demonstrating progress and results, received 53 percent more in contributions compared with organizations that are less transparent."[49]

In this case, transparency helps you create financial stability for yourself and your funded partners. When the powers that be are making decisions on budget allocations, you'll be at the top of their mind (or as the kids are saying, you'll take up residence in their minds "rent-free"). After assisting many of our Clear Impact funder clients to implement public data dashboards, many have been able to attract more funding due to transparent performance management and reporting. They've also reported increased buy-in for training and capacity-building with the people that they fund.

Remember the importance of urgency that I talked about back in Chapter 2, from the Theory of Aligned Contributions? Publishing population-level data can foster a greater sense of urgency around important community issues. It will ensure that "sunlight" is evenly distributed across the issues the community is facing. Perhaps your Common Purpose is trending in a terrible direction. Or maybe there are huge racial disparities. By sharing the data publicly, regardless of what it is, people who are already aligned with your Common Purpose may rush to join you in creating the solution. Increased awareness will grow the potential pool of resources, skills, and knowledge you can draw from.

With all that being said, you can't just post the data and expect anything to happen. You must provide narrative and help people understand that improving it is a collaborative endeavor — you can't do it all alone.

---

49 https://www.captrust.com/transparent-reputations-and-nonprofit-organizations/

Communicate how their participation will directly benefit everyone's well-being, including their own. And offer multiple ways they can participate (providing their time, money, skills, assets, connections, etc.). If another organization down the street understands your contribution to a Common Purpose, they're going to be more likely to want to engage you in working together. And maybe they'll think of innovative, creative ways that you'd never imagined.

While we want to practice unconditional honesty, transparency also promotes a healthy interest in presenting your best self. If you're drawing more attention to something, you'll be more acutely focused on improving it. By declaring publicly what it is you're trying to measurably improve, you're going to be driven to figure out ways to improve it. You'll want the data to look better the next time you update it, so you're going to try your best to make it happen. Be confident — you will improve as a result! And if things don't improve, readjust your eggs, redirect the sunlight, and recommit to doing better.

The Speed of Trust

The main reason data transparency is so beneficial is because it helps build trust in your organization and the people in charge. This is true whether you're performing poorly or exceptionally. In some cases, simply trying to be more transparent (and making that effort visible and vocal) is enough to measurably improve perceptions of trust in your operation. In tandem, doing the opposite — creating a vacuum of transparency — reduces trust, which can be disastrous. I'd like to spend a moment speaking more about the importance of trust with you, the funder, including trust-building behaviors to practice in all your important relationships (including those with your partners, staff, grantees, and the public). These are based on the teachings of Stephen Covey.

Stephen Covey speaks to audiences around the world about the role of trust and ethics in leadership and high-performance teams. He is the former CEO of Covey Leadership Center, the largest leadership development company in the world, author of the bestseller *The Speed of Trust*, and co-author of Amazon's #1 bestseller *Smart Trust*. In *The Speed of Trust*, Covey demonstrates that the more trust you have in a relationship, the faster you can move in creating understanding, making decisions, and achieving your goals.

If you want your grantees to authentically participate in your processes and be transparent about data and performance, you must make them feel safe in doing so (remember: psychological safety). To reduce friction and accelerate program impact, grantees must trust your intentions, processes, and methodologies for creating impact. They must also trust that poor data without context won't be the sole basis for punitive actions or funding decisions. How do you create trust? I'll outline some of the key ideas from Covey's book and trust development process below.

1. Trust is the number one leadership competency in today's workplace

"Trust is the one thing that changes everything." It's like water — without it relationships decay, projects underperform, and progress grinds to a crawl.

2. Feelings of trust are often the result of a deliberate process around creating trust

Simply attempting to create trust can often increase trust inherently.

3. Speak, behave, see

You must continually speak and behave in trusting ways in order to identify when trust is present.

4. There are true trust-building behaviors and counterfeit trust-building behaviors

There are 13 specific behaviors that lead to trust, including: talking straight, demonstrating respect, creating transparency, righting wrongs, showing loyalty, delivering results, getting better, confronting reality, clarifying expectations, practicing accountability, listening first, keeping commit-ments, and extending trust. Engaging in any of these behaviors in a coun-terfeit manner (inauthentically) can destroy trust.

5. Trust can be measured

Measuring trust is what makes strategizing around and improving trust possible. Figure out how to collect data around trust with your staff and partners in order to monitor and improve your behavior. You won't just want to measure trust, but each of the 13 trust-building behaviors.

6. Trust drives innovation

Trust leverages diversity, differences in opinion, and risk-taking, and cre-ates a learning culture by helping everyone to feel comfortable speaking up.

7. Trust transforms mere coordination and cooperation into real collaboration

Collaborative culture and behavior exist on a spectrum. The higher you move on the spectrum towards collaboration, the higher level of trust is required.

8. Trust multiplies results

People don't follow strategy, they follow leaders. High trust is a dividend; low trust is a tax. (Strategy x Execution) x Trust = Results.

The Data Monster Rears its Head — But You're Ready This Time

What if you have "bad" performance data or the numbers aren't quite where you want them? Why would you want to tell other people and risk unfair judgment? And if you do, how can you be sure it won't derail your efforts? First of all, I'd invite you to shift your perspective. Believe that there is no such thing as "bad" data. We must first practice acceptance if we wish to overcome the obstacles on our Hero's Journey. You can't fix something you refuse to acknowledge. Ask yourself: What's more important? Not looking "bad," or actually supporting and creating measurable improvements for the children and families you serve?

Besides changing your thinking, there are a few practical things that you can do to practice safe transparency:

1. Simply state — within your online data dashboard or PDF impact report — that you're sharing data in the interest of continual improvement, transparency, and collaboration.

2. Always include your Story Behind the Curve with every piece of data shared. Numbers are meaningless and more likely to be misinterpreted without context.

3. Make sure you share your plans for how to improve if the data is trending in the wrong direction. Anytime it's appropriate, explain how the data might be worse if you weren't doing what you're doing (but only if that's the truth).

4. Tell others how they can help in this effort. Provide an Action Plan.

That being said, there are some things you should avoid doing when sharing your data. First, don't let the perfect be the enemy of the good. Even if you don't have the perfect measures or Turn the Curve Plan, it's important to share what you've got, invite feedback, and improve everything over time. The more transparency, the better. But I know that financial measures might be taboo. Or there might be measures that aren't that important or non-outcome measures that may not be worth sharing. There might be classified information. This will require a cultural or organizational decision ahead of time — what will you share and what will stay private? Some stuff will always be classified, but I believe government agencies have a responsibility to share, at the very least, their performance and their improvement plans with the public. Anyone that receives public funding from the government has the same obligation.

Hero's Journey Spotlight:
Vermont Department of Health

The roots of the state of Vermont sharing data with the public began in 1995 when Secretary Con Hogan directed the development of Community Profiles of Health and Wellbeing. These Profiles were developed with the help of the RBA framework and showed "Data about conditions experienced by Vermonters to support the development of local insights, cross-sector collaboration, and action to make a measurable difference."[50] Each Profile also contained a set of Indicators at the County, District, and Hospital Service Area levels. The Profiles were originally published in a printed book and distributed annually until 2008. At that time, Secretary Hogan and Mark Friedman (creator of RBA) traveled the state to provide RBA training and introduce the Profiles. Vermont's Agency of Human Services (AHS) revived the practice of producing the Profiles in 2018 using the Clear Impact Scorecard — an online tool that encourages dynamic use and continuous improvement over time.

Led by Director of Performance Improvement Drusilla Roessle and a team of Social Sector Heroes across the organization — and building on the history of the Profiles — AHS required all of its six departments to share at least one scorecard on their public website, starting in 2016. This included the Department for Children and Families, Department of Corrections, Department of Disabilities, Aging, and Independent Living, Department of Mental Health, Department of Vermont Health Access, and Vermont Department of Health. According to AHS, the data scorecards help them demonstrate their commitment to driving and supporting outcomes-oriented and data-driven strategies at the state and local levels. Furthermore, AHS uses the data dashboards to measure, monitor, and continuously

---

50 https://humanservices.vermont.gov/our-impact/community-profiles-health-and-well-being

improve their programs with a focus on whether clients are better off. You can access each of the Departments' scorecards at SocialSectorHero.com/Resources.

Now, the Vermont Department of Health hosts 22 scorecards on their website, covering all their health focus areas. Each scorecard displays the population-level Outcomes (their version of "Results"), Indicators that they are trying to impact, and every state-funded program. And they didn't forget about the importance of context either! Every measure includes a corresponding Turn the Curve plan.

Furthermore, Vermont aggregated its statewide Outcomes into a separate scorecard for a high-level overview of their impact and success. The Statewide Population-Level Outcomes Report is Vermont's legislative strategy for embedding RBA into its practices. AHS inspired use of the scorecards by the Agency of Administration, which now has all Vermont agencies' submissions to the statewide indicator report done through a Scorecard. You can see the report and scorecard at SocialSectorHero.com/resources.

Some of the Vermont Department of Health's measurable improvements include:

- From 2014 to 2018, immunizations among children increased 22 percent from 63.2 percent to 76.8 percent of children aged 19 to 35 months[51]
- Public health funding increased 60 percent from $144 to $231 between 2017-2018 and 2019-2020[52]

---

51 https://www.americashealthrankings.org/explore/annual/measure/Overall_a/state/VT

52 https://www.americashealthrankings.org/explore/annual/measure/Overall_a/state/VT

- From 2001 to 2019, the prevalence of youth smokers reduced from 24 percent to 7 percent.[53]

On June 19, 2014, Health Commissioner Harry Chen, MD announced that Vermont had become one of the first state health departments to receive National Public Health Accreditation through the Public Health Accreditation Board (PHAB). The accreditation process has challenged the Health Department to think critically about the way they work to protect and promote the health of Vermonters. It allows them to identify processes where improvements are needed, and it has given them the opportunity to strengthen their culture of continuous quality improvement.

Where does transparency fit into the accreditation equation? Notably, Vermont Health Department's online scorecards help them fulfill PHAB's performance management system and public communications requirements. Community Health Assessments and Improvement Plans are also prerequisites for PHAB accreditation. Scorecards help the agency organize and share their State Health Improvement Plan scorecard publicly on their website so that visitors can get an overview of strategies and planned interventions designed to impact health priorities.

Public perception isn't necessarily the sword we're seeking to seize in this work. That's reserved for social impact. But perception can certainly influence your ability to continue providing services that are creating measurable impact. For Vermont, honesty and transparency have translated into tangible changes in perception, buy-in for their methodology, and public support.

Vermont is consistently ranked as one of the healthiest (and sometimes happiest) states in the nation. In 2017, Vermont tied with South Dakota for the top spot in the Gallup-Sharecare 2017 State of American

---

53 https://www.healthvermont.gov/about/performance/state-health-improvement-plan-2013-2017

Wellbeing Rankings, with high scores for physical health, social connections, finances, community, and sense of purpose. From 2002 to 2017, The United Health Foundation ranked Vermont in the top five overall healthiest states (they ranked first for four of those years, and ranked second in 2017).

Clearly, using scorecards to monitor performance and communicate with the public wasn't just a feel-good exercise for Vermont. Besides achieving measurable progress thanks to an enhanced focus on the data, they've reached new heights of national recognition, allowing them to increase their capacity to improve health and wellbeing for more Vermonters.

Building Your Dashboard

My goal thus far has been to convince you to share your Performance Measures and Indicators publicly on your website. Let's say I've achieved my goal. You may be wondering, how exactly do you go about doing that in an effective way? How do you build transparency that doesn't leave you vulnerable and earns you all those great outcomes I mentioned earlier? The best way to share your data publicly is to make a dedicated page on your website. Many of our clients call that particular page "Our Impact." On that page, you can present your data and Turn the Curve Plans for improvement.

In terms of structure, I recommend that you first lay out your Common Purpose in the form of Indicators (measures of community wellbeing) organized by Result areas (or goals, missions, outcomes, etc.). Let's say that your Result is "All children live prosperously" or "All children get regular physical activity." Plainly state that at the top of your report. Underneath, you'll have Indicators like "Percentage of children across the entire county regularly participating in sports." Next, you'll organize and name your programs underneath the Result and Indicator(s) they contribute to. Underneath that, you'll post the data for aggregated Performance Measures for each program. These are things like "Number of children served" or "Average cost per child served." And don't forget your better-off measures! These are things like "Percentage of children with improved GPAs" or "Average body mass index." Finally, underneath each measure, include your Story Behind the Curve, Partners, What Works strategies, and Action Plan for improvement. For an example of this structure in action, visit SocialSectorHero.com/Resources.

Once you have everything laid out in a visually appealing format on a dedicated webpage, you can simply share the link with your email list, funders, and staff. If you're a grantee, you can also take the initiative to share the public report with your funders and request a meeting for discussion. Just say, "Hey, here's our performance over the last year or month. We'd love to talk to you about it, what it means, what our plans for improvement are, and how your resources could really help make it happen." Your reports can be a compelling conversation starter if you have an eye for design. For general fundraising efforts, your public reports will be ideal content to build awareness on social media. Post an image of the graph and a link to your report and say, "Help us serve 5000 more kids this winter by donating 50 bucks."

Technology — It's Not for the Birds

Ostriches aren't the only poor creatures we've slandered because we didn't understand what they were doing. Have you ever said or heard the phrase, "That's for the birds"? It means that the topic in question is meaningless — a waste of time and energy — or something only a silly person would care about. Where did this come from? Well, back during the Second World War, some American soldiers witnessed some birds pecking around in horse manure. Seems like a disgusting waste of time right? Wrong again! Apparently, there are delicious and nutritious seeds left behind after a horse eats apples and other fruit.

You could certainly do all your performance management, reporting, and sharing manually. Lots of organizations do that. I certainly had success with it when I did fundraising for the Long Branch Athletic Association 20 years ago. But it's not 2003 anymore. There are so many software systems and tools available. When catered to your needs, technology can expedite and automate the more mundane parts of the work so that you can focus more on what matters most — seizing your sword. I know researching software companies can sometimes feel like you're a bird pecking around in manure. It takes a lot of time and convincing to get others to help you... but it's totally worth it once you find your apple seed.

The primary benefit of performance management and reporting technology is that it allows you to organize, navigate, and analyze your data much more quickly than you could without it. Second, it allows you to embed data on your website without having to manually update your website code every time a number changes. Every time you update your system, it should automatically update the data on your website. Technology can also make the task of visual data presentation quicker and easier. Finally, software reduces formatting and data-entry errors, ensuring consistency and accuracy throughout.

With advanced performance management technology, you might not be saving money, but you'll be saving time. And at the end of the day time equals money, right? So maybe we have the wrong perspective — you are saving money by accelerating your ability to make effective decisions and achieve measurable results. Because time should also bring progress and results.

What to Look for in a Performance Software Solution

Not all performance technology is built the same. If you're not careful, you could actually achieve the opposite of what you intended when implementing your system — wasted time, increased confusion, less engagement, and waning commitment.

So what should you look for when looking for a system? Below, I'll provide a list to help you navigate the research phase. This list isn't extensive and may not account for everyone's unique needs, but it's a starting point.

When you begin your software search and start preparing for demonstrations with sales staff, try editing the list to fit your needs and then email it to your point of contact so they know exactly what you're looking for. You can then grade each provider according to how well they adhere to your list of requirements. And don't take yes for an answer — ask them to *show* you how they fulfill the requirement if time allows during your demonstration. It may be worth scheduling additional meetings with more of your staff members to get all your questions answered, and the vendor should be happy to do this.

Your system should allow you to:

1. Clearly distinguish between your Common Purpose and your grantees' performance

2. Provide qualitative context (Story Behind the Curve) with every measure

3. Share your data publicly with the click of a button, a link, or a code to put on your website

4. View data trends over time periods that make sense for you (daily, weekly, monthly, quarterly, annually, etc.)

5. Analyze your data in graphs and quickly spot areas of improvement using color bands, trendlines, forecasts, or baseline percentage changes

6. Disaggregate your data by chosen subpopulations to promote equity

7. Quickly set it up with minimal training

8. If training is essential, you should be able to access it for free within the system, or the company should offer advanced training and support packages at an affordable price

9. Completely customize the language you want to use. You should be able to edit certain elements of the system,

including the name of different types of measures so that you don't have to force people to learn a whole new language just to understand the system

10. Be Section 508 compliant. You want to make sure that the report can be read by people who have a visual impairment

11. Not look messy or make your eyes go crazy trying to figure out where to look first. If you're sharing multiple measures all at once, you're going to want a clean way of looking at them and being able to click in for more information if you want it

12. Export your reports and graphs in image or PDF formats that look appealing

13. Have multiple people using the system with customizable permissions

14. Automatically collect data from your funded partners and aggregate it into measures for similar programs.

Hero's Journey Spotlight: SisterWeb

On the other side of the funding fence is grantee SisterWeb, a small community nonprofit based in San Francisco, California. SisterWeb consists of a network of culturally harmonious Doulas and birth workers belonging to and serving Black, Pacific Islander, and Latinx communities, as these ethnic and cultural groups face the most health disparities in San Francisco. SisterWeb also works to dismantle racist health care systems, strengthen community resilience, and advance economic justice for birthing families and Doulas. As of 2020, they had 26 staff and received a combined $1,248,904 in funding. Some of SisterWeb's notable funders include Every Mother Counts, San Francisco Public Health Foundation, San Francisco Health Plan, The San Francisco Foundation, Anthem Blue Shield, Merck for Mothers Safer Cities, and The University of California Berkeley.

In December 2018, The San Francisco Foundation awarded SisterWeb seed funding, and they opened three months later in March 2019. SisterWeb truly started from nothing. They were not an existing program, an extension of another program, part of a city department, or part of anything with infrastructure. Despite these modest beginnings, SisterWeb has become a powerhouse of data collection, data-based decision-making, and data transparency. As part of their funding, they were paired with an evaluations team from UC Berkeley who helped them understand the importance of data collection, how to tell important stories through numbers, and how to use ethical data collection methods.

Originally, SisterWeb utilized Google forms to collect their client-level data, but ultimately it wasn't secure enough for their needs. They also tested out medical provider platforms, but these systems only collected and stored data — there was no way to practice data evaluation, track progress over time, or share achievements with partners and the public. Like our friends the birds — they were pecking through the manure but they hadn't found the apple seed yet. But, with a little assistance, a few tools helped them find their way.

A few years ago, SisterWeb's co-founder and Director of Evaluations Alli Cuentos came across *Trying Hard is Not Good Enough* and the RBA framework. Alli convinced Marna Armstead, SisterWeb's Executive Director, to crawl out from under her mountain of paperwork and read the book. Marna fell in love and began using RBA to direct the organization. She loved RBA's plain-speaking approach to nonprofit work, and a common language helped SisterWeb remain transparent with its staff and the public throughout its organizational processes. Additionally, RBA proved to be adaptable from SisterWeb's "low-tech/no-tech situation" to their current level of technological sophistication in using Clear Impact's data collection and evaluation systems.

RBA also created an impetus for SisterWeb to transparently share its progress with staff and the public. Motivated by attracting more funding from existing and new funders, they began to read up on the benefits of sharing data and pecking around for systems to help them do it effectively. Eventually, Marna came across the Clear Impact Scorecard and thought, "I want a Scorecard on our website!" Marna also found that Compyle (Scorecard's sister data-collection system) was the answer to their data collection needs.

A year after embarking on its RBA and technology journey, SisterWeb had established its Common Purpose in the form of four overarching goals and accompanying Indicators all managed in online scorecards. They collect their data through surveys, put it into spreadsheets that are sorted and disaggregated, analyze and reflect on the data, and review it in supervision meetings. Throughout all their data collection efforts, SisterWeb ensures that everyone has access to the data they need to make good decisions about their work. Part of this effort is the intentional involvement of all SisterWeb's Directors in data collection and entry — each Director is responsible for managing a particular set of data.

To enhance collaboration, SisterWeb regularly distributes data reports to each of its programs so that each can stay current on SisterWeb's goals, the state of community Indicators, areas of progress, and challenges. Data is thus made highly visible, always adhering to ethical guidelines and striking a balance between numbers and narrative. But, SisterWeb understands that transparency isn't the endgame — it's a means to continual improvement, buy-in, and capacity-building. After distributing data reports, SisterWeb solicits feedback on what might be missing from the story. All staff are free to request particular reports or data. Not only does this help everyone stay aligned — it contributes to a feeling of belonging and that the organization cares for its staff and Doulas. As of 2020, 85 percent of Doulas felt that SisterWeb cared about helping them achieve their professional goals, and they continue to work on Turning the Curve.

Transparency isn't just an internal game for SisterWeb. They use RBA and public scorecards to uplift their work and draw attention to the needs and changes that arise as part of a growing, learning organization. Each of their four organizational goals is publicly displayed on their website via an "Our Impact" page, and each button links to a performance scorecard. In addition to scorecards, the webpage houses an interactive Annual Report, notable measurable accomplishments, and a financial snapshot disclosing where funding comes from and where it goes (down to the exact dollar amount!).

On SisterWeb's "Our Impact" webpage, visitors can see the current status of health Indicators for each of the organizational goals (to be updated by late 2022):

- **Goal 1:** SisterWeb nurtures a skilled workforce of Community Doulas who see birth work as a viable profession

- **Goal 2:** SisterWeb's culturally congruent, holistic Doula care supports Black, Native Hawaiian Pacific Islander, and Latinx pregnant and birthing people in achieving their own birth goals

- **Goal 3:** SisterWeb engages in the national movement to eliminate structural racism in healthcare systems as a driver of birth inequities

- **Goal 4:** SisterWeb expands and strengthens its operational effectiveness and organizational sustainability.

You can view these Scorecards at SocialSectorHero.com/Resources.

The early implementation of RBA and efforts around data transparency set SisterWeb up for exponential growth. These efforts allowed them to engage partners in discovering issues and making changes on the fly. Recently, they transitioned 10 Doulas from independent contractors to full-time employees with benefits. In 2020 SisterWeb reported that 100 percent of their Doula client survey respondents reported that SisterWeb's services helped them achieve their birthing goals, feel more confident in navigating healthcare systems, and feel more connected to their body.

When it comes to developing a world-class performance reporting and data transparency system that works for grantees, Marna has a few recommendations for funders:

- Pour development and resources into how organizations can carry out their data development agenda, including staffing, technology, tools, and general operations

- Use targets and Indicators that are fair and useful

- Provide ongoing technical support for the implementation of technology

- Account and plan for the extensive time it may take for grantees to customize and make data collection meaningful.

CHAPTER 9 ACTION PLAN

1. Identify the measures and Turn the Curve Plans you want to share externally

2. Research software vendors that can help you automate your performance management and reporting process and request a few demos. The Clear Impact Scorecard is one system you may want to consider.

3. Copy the list of "Your system should allow you to" recommendations earlier in this chapter and put it into a Word Document. Choose what you want to keep and edit the list to add any other features you're looking for. Send that list to your potential vendors.

4. Check out the SisterWeb and the Vermont Agency of Human Services Scorecards at SocialSectorHero.com/Resources to see if that's something that you might want to emulate.

CHAPTER 10:
THE ADVENTURE CONTINUES

The Hero's Journey is Cyclical

Remember the traditional hero's journey we explored in some of the previous chapters? In many stories, the last stage of this journey involves the hero making the journey back home after they've seized their sword or vanquished their foe. Upon their return, they are able to join in celebration with their fellow heroes and village mates and enjoy the next epoch of peace. For you and your grantees, celebration is equally important. Don't forget to integrate celebration and recognition for your partners throughout your journey. It will help you maintain momentum and reinforce behaviors and actions that lead to measurable progress.

A Social Sector Hero deserves to enjoy the triumphs and treasures of their journey — but the adventure is rarely complete after the first iteration. Once your social sector fellowship seizes its sword or Turns the Curve on Indicator(s) and/or Performance Measure(s), you can't become complacent. The work of a hero is never done, nor is your social impact adventure. There will always be another mountain peak to climb, treasure to find, or foe to vanquish.

Harking back to Chapter Eight, continual dialogue is the water source that will sustain your adventure so you can emerge from proverbial deserts, reach new heights, explore new frontiers for impact, and continue to achieve measurable results. Environmental and social conditions are in a perpetual state of change. Stories Behind the Curve may change over time. And if you're not conscious of this, the data troll might trick you again. What gets attention gets done. And if you're not focused on continual progress, the data will inevitably start to trend in the wrong direction. The social impact journey is an ongoing, iterative process that is never over.

Continual dialogue won't just prevent regression in the data — it can also ensure your Curve stays Turned, getting you ever closer to your target and beyond. Say you're looking at a high school graduation rate (or any Indicator that's meaningful to you). Over the span of five years your social impact fellowship uses the strategies in this book to improve the measure by 25 percent. It's gone from 68 percent to 93 percent. That's a really high graduation rate. You might be thinking, "What else could I possibly do to improve this further?" Always return to effective dialogue!

Here's a list of things you can do at your next Turn the Curve, performance, or 1x4 meeting to help you sustain and accelerate your Turned Curves:

1. Explore existing and new limiting factors

2. Consider if there are any feasible new What Works strategies that you didn't have time or capacity to try before

3. Prioritize completing actions in the Action Plan that have yet to be started or completed

4. Consider the actions that worked well and do more of them. Or, do them better

5. If you haven't done so already or don't have updated figures, disaggregate the data again and implement new strategies specific to certain subpopulations

6. Explore your assumptions again and again

7. Seek new perspectives and revisit your internal and external DEI efforts

8. Consider whether there are people you haven't talked to yet

9. Engage more community partners and stakeholders. Try focus groups or surveys

10. Ask other funders to give you feedback on your Indicator Turn the Curve Plans

11. Create peer coaching amongst grantees. Give them the platform to do so

12. Explore where there might be duplication of effort across the fellowship. Strategize how to reduce redundancy to free up time and resources for new avenues of impact

13. Consider new tools to help you improve your data management and sharing.

The Eight Core Strategies

There are eight core strategies you should take away from our journey here together. These are the underpinning principles of my approach to funding for social change. When implemented in tandem, these core strategies can help you make better funding decisions, collaborate better with your grantees, create a world-class performance reporting system, and realize your social impact destiny. I'll briefly summarize them again here:

1. Align With a Common Purpose

Key Ideas:

- To achieve real, measurable impact, you and your grantees must not act as individual superstars, but create a cohesive front through a Common Purpose, shared strategies, and disciplined measurement.

- **A Common Purpose** = Result(s) + Indicator(s) that you share among your partners and utilize to guide all strategies and activities.

- Give yourself permission to engage in "action learning." Learn and act as you go rather than delaying things until you have the perfect plan.

2. Ensure Alignment Throughout Your Journey

Key Ideas:

- Designing your Common Purpose is only half the battle. You must continually ensure that you hold yourself and your partners accountable for "living" the Common Purpose through aligned measurement and strategies.

- Creating alignment starts with defining one Result and a maximum of five Indicators that quantify the achievement of the Result.

- At the very least, you should sit down once a year for one hour to discuss progress on one metric with one grantee at a time (1x4 meeting).

3. Remember, Less is More

Key Ideas:

- Avoid engaging in any extraneous activities and/or collecting unhelpful data that distracts you from your most important mission.

- To maintain alignment, you should have every funded partner report on a maximum of five Performance Measures. The metrics should be designed around the Common Purpose and primarily speak to whether each partner's clients are better off as a result of their programs and services.

- Results-Based Accountability's Turn the Curve Thinking process is a logical, common-sense approach to analyzing and improving your Indicators and Performance Measures. It is the single most important tool to help you and your grantees realize your social sector destiny.

4. Disaggregate Your Data for True Understanding

Key Ideas:

- Only looking at data "totals" can cause you to act on faulty, or even dangerous, assumptions. You must disaggregate your data by race, gender, age, or any other factors to truly understand the state of wellbeing in your community.

- The main purpose of disaggregating data is to unveil disparities so that your strategies are appropriately designed to address root causes for specific subpopulations.

- Disparities are intersectional in nature. When disaggregating your data, consider disaggregating by two levels for a deeper understanding (e.g. look at what's happening to women of a particular race, in addition to looking at all genders in total).

5. Be Consistent and Flexible

Key Ideas:

- Your funded partners need consistency *and* flexibility to achieve success. The main way to do this is to establish a handful of similar measures for each comparable set of programs, but also to allow grantees to report on a handful of optional measures that speak to their unique circumstances.

- Every one of your grantees should be using the same Data Management System to report data to you. This will allow for better analysis between similar programs and improve the navigation and organization of your data.

- As much as humanly possible, make sure everyone in your social sector fellowship is utilizing the same language and frameworks so you can compare apples to apples.

6. Never Report on Data Without the Story

Key Ideas:

- Data without context is meaningless. To make effective investment decisions and create strategies that actually work, you must analyze the root causes behind the state of the data. This requires a diverse audience to explore contributing and limiting factors.

- Just because a data trendline isn't where you want it to be, this does not equal "bad" performance. Even with a heroic effort, progress can stall or regress. Make sure you consider external factors before making rash decisions or budget cuts.

- Never ask grantees to report on data without a narrative or Story Behind the Curve.

7.Support Effective Dialogue

Key Ideas:

- To navigate data pitfalls (e.g. misleading data) and get closer to capturing the object of your quest, the most important tool you have at your disposal is effective dialogue.

- **Effective Dialogue** = communication, guided by effective questions and deep listening, among two or more parties, that results in increased understanding and an action plan.

- Asking your grantees the right questions allows them to surface information, challenges, and needs you can help them to address. Consider utilizing the list of Effective Questions in Chapter Eight, based on the work of Doug Krug, to guide your Turn the Curve conversations with grantees.

8. Report Your Data Publicly

Key Ideas:

- Sharing your Indicator and Performance data publicly can create greater alignment, stoke urgency for your cause, build trusting relationships, invite more funding, and foster collaboration for results.

- **Practicing Transparency** = clearly communicating your data, your thinking and analysis, and your improvement plans in an easily accessible location, using plain language, formatted for anyone to see and understand.

- When catered to your needs, technology can expedite and automate the more mundane parts of data entry and analysis so that you can focus more on what matters most — seizing your sword. Performance reporting software can help you organize, navigate, and analyze your data quicker and easier. It also makes it easier to share your data publicly and update it.

A Hero Accepts Guidance

While I was writing this book, I interviewed many Social Sector Heroes to develop the amazing case studies shared with you here. They also offered invaluable insights and feedback in shaping the eight core strategies. If there's one final thing you take away from our Social Sector Hero Journey Spotlights, it's to recognize when you might need more help. While most of the strategies here are common sense, sometimes implementation can get confusing. Maybe you'd like to learn more about the Results-Based Accountability framework. Maybe you're at the stage where you're considering finding a Unified Data Management system. Maybe you love some of the ideas, but you're not sure where to get started.

Wherever you are in your journey, finding a partner invested in your success can accelerate your results far beyond what you thought possible. Working with people with proven expertise in performance management systems, social impact, collaboration, and effective investing can pay for itself in measurable gains. While there is a cost, engaging experts early on can help you save time, energy, and resources down the road.

That being said, if you'd be interested in working together to implement any of the eight core strategies, I'm happy to invite you to email me at Adam@ClearImpact.com. You can also book a free 20-minute discovery call with me at SocialSectorHero.com/Discovery to:

1. Learn more about how to implement the strategies in this book

2. Learn about consulting and technical assistance options

3. Learn more about how to use technology to organize, analyze, improve, and share your data.

In doing so, as part of the discovery call, I will also create a **Social Sector Hero Rating and Report**, that will be customized to your organization and sent to you after the call. This rating and report can be used for you to understand where you are in the Social Sector Hero's journey and recommendations on next steps.

Clear Impact offers funders performance management training, along with services and software to help them track the performance of programs, measure the impact of investments, and report on the progress of missions. We work side-by-side with you to establish measurable performance expectations, identify the right data Indicators and continuously monitor your progress through proven frameworks and processes to deliver long-term, measurable impact. We take on a limited number of clients each year to provide exceptional service and we work with organizations committed to public transparency, accountability for results, and continuous improvement. If this sounds like you, please do not hesitate to contact me or visit our website at ClearImpact.com.

Now, I offer to you my deepest and most sincere congratulations! By finishing this book, you have taken a giant step forward on your Social Sector Hero's journey to measurable impact. I hope you have found this book to be a valuable map and inspiring resource. If you know any other Social Sector Heroes who might benefit from reading this book, please let me know at Adam@ClearImpact.com and I'll personally send them an invitation to read the book.

I look forward to hearing from you and wish you safe travels on the path to your mountain peak.

ACKNOWLEDGEMENTS

First and foremost, I need to acknowledge Kayleigh Weaver, Clear Impact Communications Manager. Without her, most of the ideas and stories in this book would still be in my head. Her creativity and writing talent helped to make what is generally considered to be a boring topic — performance reporting — into something fun to read. Kayleigh deserves 90 percent of the credit on this book.

I need to thank all the Social Sector Heroes that were interviewed and provided feedback on their stories. They include (in order they appear in the book) Kim Malat, Karen Finn, Dan Duncan, Ada Freund, Liz Cortez, Ayeola Fortune, Andrew Kleine, Isadora Delvecchio, Marcos Marquez, Amy Rydel, Tiffani Johnson, Beth Stockton, Anne McIntyre-Lahner, Julie Singley, Brenda Petell, Marian Reuter Godwin, Terie Taylor-Wolf, Jim Macrae, Drusilla Roessle, and Marna Armstead.

I'd like to express my gratitude for my long-time dear friend and colleague Dr. JaNay Queen Nazaire for the thoughtful and inspiring foreword.

I also want to thank the Clear Impact Leadership Team of Kara Barnes, Travis Bechthold, Hana Kim and Justin Miklas for believing in this project and giving me and Kayleigh the space to finish it. Thank you to

Mark Friedman for your contribution of Results-Based Accountability to the world and for being a mentor and friend from the beginning.

Thank you to my wife and kids for letting me tell their stories as part of the book even if some may be considered "embarrassing." This journey would not be the same without your daily love and support.

Lastly, thank you to the readers who are committed to improving the lives of children, families and communities and for helping to promote readership across your networks.